God Has Never Failed Me, But He Sure Has Scared Me to Death a Few Times!

by
Dr. Stan Toler

#9586

Honor Books
Tulsa, Oklahoma

God Has Never Failed Me, But He Sure Has Scared Me To Death a Few Times!
ISBN 1-56292-130-4
Copyright © 1995 by Stan Toler

Published by HONOR BOOKS
P.O. Box 55388
Tulsa, Oklahoma 74155

Dedication

To my mother, Loretta, who taught me at an early age the importance of a relationship with Jesus Christ.

"Be strong and courageous. Do not be afraid or terrified because of them, for the Lord your God goes with you; he will never leave you nor forsake you" Deuteronomy 31:6.

Contents

Acknowledgements

Special thanks...

To Barbara Johnson, for encouraging me to write this book and to stick with my title.

To Jim Wilcox, the SNU "Grammar Hammer," tennis partner, and the man with the red pen for wise editorial guidance and helpful suggestions.

To Mechelle Fain, for countless hours in front of a computer typing and re–typing the manuscript. Bless you for your ability to read my handwriting!

To Derl Keefer, for research assistance and creative ideas.

To Mom, Dad, Terry, and Mark — I love you more than words can express.

To all sources unknown — I would love to give credit where credit is due, but after nearly 30 years of ministry, I don't remember. Let me know, and I will credit you in the next printing.

To my wife, Linda, for reading rough draft chapters and for verifying the accuracy of my stories.

To Talmadge Johnson, "G.I. Barber," brother beloved. Thanks for your confidence in me.

To Charles Wetzel, for insightful suggestions and content review.

To my sons, Seth and Adam, for giving me permission to tell your stories (they actually served as proofreaders!)

To the INJOY leadership team, John Maxwell, and Dick Peterson. Thanks for believing in me!

To Keith Provance and the Honor Book family. Thanks for everything!

You are loved,

Stan Toler
Ephesians 3:20,21

Foreword

The title of this book would make a best seller even if the material were not captivating. Stan has the ability to bond laughter with the solid truth of the Scriptures so that I felt that bubble of joy erupt as he describes incidents of God's faithfulness.

With the story in Chapter One about God's provision for us, I sensed that warm — fuzzy — wrapping that God does for us when He drops His canvas of love over us. Sometimes we are more aware of it than other times.

The sparkling stories of incidents which reveal God's care for us come through so clearly in Stan's writing. Somehow the small, almost trite situations shine through and become like lights brightly outlining a darkened pathway.

Stan's book is such an encouragement even in heavy circumstances, reminding us that He did not begin to love us because of what we were, and He will go on loving us in spite of what we are. The grace of God is so poured out on us with Stan's wise counsel.

We know the word *encourage* means "to fill the heart," and Stan does a superb job of using the scripture plus anecdotes to truly fill the heart. The blend that is in the book of spiritual truths — plus insights learned from a life of service to God — makes this book rich in wisdom and exhortation.

I recently started a collection of angels, such as Gabriel holding up his trumpet to blow. After reading this book, I went out and bought four more angels to place around my home just to remind me that hope is ahead for us. We have an *endless hope*, not a *hopeless end*, and Stan's book was such a challenge for me to keep that thought eminent: looking for His blessed appearing.

Joyfully, with love,
Barbara Johnson

Preface

Anyone who first meets Stan Toler knows immediately that he is an original. No one else I know has the same kind of wit, charm, and positive outlook on life that he does. And he is also one of the funniest men I have ever met. Stan has the uncanny ability to see the humor in any situation, capture it in his imagination, and then recount it with grace and style of a southern storyteller. I have been glad to call Stan my good friend and colleague for more than 25 years.

What you cannot tell when you first meet Stan is that he has experienced some genuinely difficult times, times that would knock the humor out of someone else the way the wind gets knocked out of you when you land flat on your back.

Stan has the unsinkable spirit. He also possesses keen insight. In this book, he shares many of his observations and insights — loaded with humor, of course. You will find yourself laughing one minute and crying the next. In the end, you will come to share his outlook. You will begin to see humor in life's circumstances. And as Scripture says, A merry heart doeth good like a medicine Proverbs 17:22.

John C. Maxwell
San Diego, California

Introduction

The first time I heard Barbara Johnson speak, I was moved to tears as she shared the setbacks she had encountered in life. Barbara unfolded the story of her son Steven being killed in an ambush near DaNang. She told of the tragic death of another son, Tim, who was killed five years later in a head–on collision with a drunk driver. She spoke of the depression that swept over her when her third son, Larry, met her at the flagpole in Disneyland and declared, "Mom, I'm a homosexual." I thought, what a tough lady! Barbara then said something that tore me up, "Laughter is in nationwide demand!" From that moment forward, this lady who had been through so much knocked me off my seat with humor.

After church, we went to Shoney's for dinner. "Barbara," I said, "I've been thinking about writing a book."

She said, "Tell me about your book title."

It was an important question coming from a person who had written such exciting books as, *Pack Up Your Gloomies in a Great Big Box, Then Sit on the Lid and Laugh!; Splashes of Joy in the Cesspools of Life;* and *Mama, Get the Hammer! There's a Fly on Papa's Head.*

"OK," I said, "here goes: *God's Never Failed Me, But He Sure Has Scared Me to Death a Few Times!*" She nearly fell over laughing! "Don't let anyone talk you out of that title — it's wonderful!" she said.

So I began writing and reflecting on my relationship with the Lord during almost 30 years in the ministry.

This is a book about the faithfulness of God. Within its pages, you will find inspirational and humorous stories of God's power at work in the world.

Leslie Miller, in the *USA Today* newspaper, recently stated, "When it comes to religion, the USA is a land of believers. A new *USA Today*/CNN/Gallup Poll reveals that 96 percent of Americans believe in God."[1]

With this startling report, perhaps J.I. Packer was right when he said, "Our expectations with regard to seeing the power of God transforming people's lives are not as high as they should be."

As a young teen attending the Fifth Avenue Church in Columbus, Ohio, I often heard my pastor, the Rev. C.O. Walters, ask the question, "Is everybody happy? If so, say Amen!" What an impact this had on my spiritual life. A minister who believes in laughter!

This reminds me of the 3-year-old boy who listened attentively to the Sunday morning message. When asked about what he had learned, the little boy responded, "Jesus died so that we could have ever–laughing life!" And you know what? He is right! Salvation and everlasting life include joy and laughter.

Oswald Chambers called humor "the lubricant of missionary life." It is my belief that laughter is very much a part of my faith life. When we dismiss laughter from the pulpit, the pew, and every day life, we miss God's best for us in Christian experiences.

Humor is to life what shock absorbers
are to automobiles

My simple faith in God's ability to perform miracles was often encouraged by the words affixed to the wall in the choir loft of my home church: "Jesus Never Fails." I accepted this at face value and have never ceased to believe that "God can do anything but fail!"

It is my prayer that this book will inspire many to renew their faith in God's ability to do the impossible. May the words of the prophet Isaiah challenge your faith and calm your fears.

Fear not, for I have redeemed you; I have called you by name; you are mine. When you pass through the waters, I will be with you; and when you pass through the rivers, they will not sweep over you. When you walk through the fire, you will not be burned; the flames will not set you ablaze. For I am the Lord, your God, the Holy One of Israel, your Savior; I give Egypt for your ransom, Cush and Seba in your stead. Since you are precious and honored in my sight, and because I love you, I will give men in exchange for your life. Do not be afraid, for I am with you; I will bring your children from the east and gather you from the west Isaiah 43:1-5.

---

[1]Leslie Miller, *USA Today*, December 21, 1994.

1

Pinto Beans and Fried Bologna
Create a Feast of Faith

"...we do not know what to do!"
2 Chronicles 20:12

Growing up in the hills of West Virginia was a delightful experience. My dad was a coal miner, and we lived in a coal mining community—Baileysville (unincorporated). Of course, most towns in West Virginia are still unincorporated. In fact, the population of Baileysville is down to 60 as of 1994, so it will never be incorporated! But it is my hometown! Californians love to brag about being able to go to the mountains to snow ski and the ocean to sun bathe in the same day. Well, in Baileysville, if you lived on the side of the mountain, you could cross the river any day, any time, on an old–fashioned swinging bridge!

My Saturdays were spent at the Wyoming Company Store. While Mom and Dad made purchases with coal mining dollars, I was in charge of watching my brothers, Terry and Mark. Of course, it wasn't difficult. We eagerly peered at the black and white television sets in the furniture department. Programs such as "Fury," "Sky King," and "My Friend Flicka" seemed so real!

Our small white frame house was located on the side of Baileysville Mountain. We had a well nearby that provided ample water and a pot–bellied coal stove to keep us warm (as long as you remembered to put coal in it!).

I have heard that someone is a "redneck" if his bathroom requires a flashlight and shoes; well, our little house had three rooms and a bath but it was our home, and I loved it no matter how pink it made my neck. One of the saddest days of my childhood was a Saturday morning when we returned home from a visit to the company store and saw our tiny home engulfed in flames. We lost everything, and I cried for days.

Years later, Pastor Richard Grindstaff told us that as the house burned to the ground, Dad put his arm around him and said, "The Lord giveth and the Lord taketh away. Blessed be the name of the Lord!"

By the time I was 11 years old, we had moved to Columbus, Ohio, in search of a better life. My dad, only 31 years old, had already broken his back three times in the coal mines and was suffering from the dreaded miners' disease, "black lung." But we were happy and almost always had pinto beans, cornbread, and fried bologna for supper. (That's right, only later did it become *dinner!*)

Christmas Day, 1961, will always be one of the most wonderful, life–changing days for me. It had been a long hard winter with lots of snow and cold weather. Times were tough! Dad had been laid off from construction work, our food supply had dwindled to nothing, and we had closed off most of the house in order to cut down our high utility bills.

This epiphany really began Christmas Eve when Mom noted that we had no food for Christmas Day and no hope of getting any. That was difficult for me to understand. We were used to Mom's calling out, "Pinto beans, cornbread, and fried bologna. Come and get it!" But now there was nothing in the house! Mom suggested that it was time for us to accept a handout from the government commoditive department, so reluctantly Dad loaded Terry, Mark, and I into our old Plymouth, and we headed downtown. When we got there, we stood in line with hundreds of others for what seemed like hours, waiting for government handouts of cheese, dried milk, flour, and dried eggs. Ugh! The air was cold, and the snow was blowing as we stood there shivering. Finally, Dad could stand it no longer.

"We're going home, boys. God will provide!" he said. We cried, but trusted Dad's faith in God completely.

That night, we popped popcorn and opened gifts that we had ordered with Top Value trading stamps which Mom had saved for Christmas gifts. Perhaps some of you are too young to remember Top Value stamps. Almost all grocery stores gave out stamps for purchases made. You could save the stamps and fill up Top Value Books for redemption. In my day, Top Value provided a catalog that listed the number of books needed for a gift item. So Mom saved stamps all year long, counted the bounty by November 1, and let the Toler boys pick out their Christmas presents.

Terry got a transistor radio. (He hadn't even realized that we had no money to purchase a battery!) I had ordered a miniature Brownie Kodak camera (not smart, since we couldn't afford film, either!) And baby brother Mark got a small teddy bear. While none of the gifts was a surprise to us, Mom had carefully and lovingly wrapped each one to be opened Christmas Eve. We were grateful to have anything!

Everyone slept well under Grandma Brewster's handmade quilts that night. While we were fearful of the next day without food, we were just happy to be together as a family. (Little did we know that Dad would be in Heaven by the next Christmas.)

On Christmas morning, December 25, 1961, we were all asleep in Mom and Dad's bedroom. Suddenly, we were startled by a loud knock and a hearty "Merry Christmas!" greeting from people who attended the Fifth Avenue Church. There stood Clair Parsons, Dalmus Bullock, and others with gifts, clothes, and a 30-day supply of food. (Yes, dried pinto beans, cornmeal, and a huge roll of bologna were included!) Since that day, I have always believed that God will provide, and that God is *never late* when we need a miracle!

"We must bring the presence of God into our families.
And how do we do that? By praying."

Mother Teresa
Nobel Laureate

In 2 Chronicles 20:12, one of my favorite Bible stories comes to life when King Jehoshaphat cries out to God, "Our God...we have no power...we do not know what to do!" King Jehoshaphat had just discovered three new enemies. Unfortunately, all three were lined up against the tiny nation of Israel, and King Jehoshaphat realized that he was powerless without God's help.

The scene was not unlike the Toler home. King Jehoshaphat was in what appeared to be a hopeless situation. As we continue reading, we learn that King Jehoshaphat leads the children of Israel in divinely directed steps to a miraculous intervention from God above.

Seek the Lord

"Alarmed, Jehoshaphat resolved to inquire of the Lord" (v. 3).

"And he proclaimed a fast for all Judah and the people of Judah came together to seek help from the Lord (v. 4).

In verse 6, he asks God a significant question: "Are you not God in heaven?" In other words, he is saying, "God, if You can take care of this universe and bring order to it, then You can provide for me."

He asks God another question in verse 7: "Did you not drive out the inhabitants of this land?" He is reminding himself of God's faithfulness in the past. I am beginning to realize that my faith today anchors to the faith that my Dad passed on to me with his wisdom: "God will provide." And provide He did for the Tolers! After Dad's death, God sent a wonderful Kentucky stepfather, Jack Hollingsworth, into our lives. He saw to it that each son of William Aaron Toler had plenty of pinto beans, fried bologna (he is an expert at cooking it!), cornbread, and a college education; all three boys later became Nazarene ministers.

Confess Your Need

"We are powerless against the great multitude that is coming against us" (v. 12). If you want God's help, you must confess your need! The world in which we live is a world of independence. We are taught to look out for No. 1, to do our own thing, to think for ourselves, and to trust in our own abilities. King Jehoshaphat

reminded the children of Israel that "Me–ism" won't work here! He confessed that they were inadequate against the three enemies they faced: *"In your hands, God, are power and might."* When I need God's provision, I look up and confess, "God I am incapable, but You have all the resources for my miracle!"

Focus on God, Not Your Problem

"We do not know what to do, but our eyes are on you..." (v. 12). King Jehoshaphat gave them a formula for deliverance: "Get your eyes off the problem!" Your focus must be on God!

As an adult, living in Oklahoma during tough times has also strengthened my faith in God. In the mid–1980's, I watched so many banks fail; in fact, the FDIC closed so many banks in my hometown of Oklahoma City that I wore a T–shirt that said, "I bank with FDIC!" Agriculture diminished, and oil rigs stopped pumping. But even in the most difficult situations, a simple faith in God and a calm reassurance in the face of insurmountable obstacles resulted in victory.

I will always remember sitting at a table in the Oklahoma City Marriott Hotel Restaurant on Northwest Expressway and listening to my friend, Melvin Hatley, founder of USA Waste Management Company, talk about the collapse of the oil industry and the failure of old First National Bank downtown. Tears flowed freely, and yet his faith took hold as he discussed God's history of faithfulness. His calm assurance, founded and grounded in a dynamic faith and a willingness to start over, made all the difference in his financial recovery. Today, Melvin is a testimony of the phrase, "Tough times don't last, but tough people do!"

On December 17, 1903, Wilbur and Orville Wright made history. They defied the law of gravity and flew through the air. Many forget that the concept of flying was not new with the Wright brothers. In fact, several years before the brothers flew their motorized plane at Kitty Hawk, scientists had discovered that flying was possible. While others remained skeptical, the Wright brothers believed the formulas and designed their own plane. When they achieved "first flight," they demonstrated the importance of trusting the facts and taking action in order to experience results.

The same is true for the Christian. We can know a lot about God and the Bible, but until we relax in faith and believe in the promises of God, we will be disappointed.

I love the story that my professor, Dr. Amos Henry, used to tell about D.L. Moody. Apparently, Moody was on a ship that was crossing the Atlantic Ocean one night when it caught on fire and they formed a bucket brigade to pass ocean water to the scene of the fire. One man in the line turned and said, "Mr. Moody, don't you think we should retire from the line and go down and pray?"

"You can go pray if you want to," Moody replied, " but I'm going to pray while I pass the buckets." What great insight! God wants to see if you mean business, so pray while you work!

Relax in Faith

Two men were climbing a particularly difficult mountain when one of them suddenly fell down a crevasse 500 feet deep.

"Are you all right, Bert?" called the man at the top of the crevasse.

"I'm still alive, thank goodness, Fred," came the reply.

"Here, grab this rope," said Fred, throwing a rope down to Bert.

"I can't grab it," shouted Bert. "My arms are broken."

"Well, fit it around your legs."

"I'm afraid I can't do that either," said Bert. "My legs are broken."

"Put the rope in your mouth," shouted Fred.

So Bert put the rope in his mouth and Fred began to haul him to safety. 490 feet...400 feet...300 feet...200 feet...100 feet...50 feet...and then Fred called out, "Hey Bert, how are you doing?"

Bert replied, "I'm fine...Uh oh!"

Don't let go of the rope, my friend! Dr. Steve Brown says, "Tie a knot and hang on!"

"This battle is not for you to fight. Take your position and stand still and see the victory of the Lord on your behalf" (v. 17). Verse 17 of this chapter is the middle verse of the entire Old Testament. It is like a pregnant pause for the believer. This concept, "stand still," is like going into the batter's box during a World Series baseball game with a great pitcher on the mound, digging in, and saying, "I don't care how fast you throw that ball, I'm anchored here and you can't move me!" King Jehoshaphat said, "Stand your ground but remain calm — God is going to help us."

Of course, that's easier said than done. Harmon Schmelzenbach, missionary to Africa, often holds audiences spellbound with his story about a huge python that uncoiled itself from the rafters and then wrapped itself around his body while he was kneeling to pray.

The python is known for its ability to kill its victim by squeezing it to death. Schmelzenbach stated that Isaiah 30:15, *"In repentance and rest is your salvation, in quietness and trust is your strength, but you would have none of it"* instantly flooded his mind. With the huge snake wrapped around his body, he testified that he felt the calm assurance that God was in control. Harmon remained perfectly still and prayed like never before!

If he had moved a muscle, no doubt the giant python would have constricted and killed him. Slowly, Schmelzenbach reported, the snake uncoiled itself and went back to the rafters.

We have more than 7,000 promises in Scripture to stand on. Plus, you can stand on the character of God! God has never lost a battle. Why not resign as General Manager of the Universe, eat a bowl of beans and cornbread, and relax in faith?

Give God Thanks Before Your Miracle

King Jehoshaphat began to appoint those who could sing. *"And they began to sing and praise the Lord and the Lord sent an ambush and they won the battle"* (verse 22). Do you get the picture? Three armies of blood–thirsty warriors with overwhelming strength and weaponry lined up against tiny Israel, and the King called on the choir to sing! Talk about faith. They claimed victory!

The scene was the Second World War. The British had just suffered a terrible defeat at Dunkirk, losing almost all of their military supplies during the evacuation of their soldiers. France had been conquered, and the United States had not yet entered the war. England stood as an island nation, alone against the Axis powers.

Prime Minister Winston Churchill knew he had to bolster the courage and the determination of his people. He needed to make a speech, an inspiring speech, that would rally the citizens. On Sunday evening, June 2, 1940, Churchill was in his Cabinet Room at 10 Downing Street. His secretary, Mary Shearburn, was poised at the typewriter. Dictating, Churchill paced from the fireplace to the velvet–draped windows and back again. Slowly his speech emerged onto the typed page. Often he would rip a sheet from the machine, only to begin anew. It was late, and the room was cold in the night air. The prime minister's voice had now grown hoarse and faint. His head bowed, sobbing, for he did not know what to say. Silence. A minute passed, maybe two. It seemed like an eternity. Abruptly his head rose and his voice trumpeted. He spoke as a man with authority. The thought descended upon him as from an angel above. "We shall NEVER surrender!"

Perhaps those words did come from an angel. Who knows? All we know is that God is faithful. Regardless of how scary or how seemingly hopeless our mission may be, He does not forsake us. All we have to do is trust our fears and our failures to His hands. He will not let us down.[1]

Many fears do not overwhelm Him!

Many was the day my own father lived his faith in God, trudging home in the snow from the coal mines, face darkened with coal dust, lunch bucket jangling, whistling the old tune, "His Eye Is On the Sparrow."

Why should I feel discouraged?
Why should the shadows come?
Why should my heart be lonely

And long for heaven and home?

When Jesus is my portion?

My constant friend is He.

His eye is on the sparrow,

And I know He watches me![2]

Yes, God who sits on a throne in heaven is interested in you! If He tends to the lilies of the fields and attends the funeral of a baby sparrow (and He does!), surely He will provide for you!

---

[1]King Duncan (Seven Worlds Publishers, 1993), *Parables*.

[2]Civilla D. Martin (Words: 1905) Charles H. Gabriel (Music: 1905) *"His Eye Is on The Sparrow"* (Public Domain).

2

Are You Undesirable, Unmentionable,
or Totally Undone?

"Here is a trustworthy saying that deserves full acceptance:
Christ Jesus came into the world to save sinners."
I Timothy 1:15

Florence Littauer is one of my favorite speakers. Recently, we shared speaking duties at an INJOY Church Growth Conference in Atlanta, Georgia, and as usual, Florence was winning the crowd with her great sense of humor and anecdotes of everyday life. She told one delightful story about a speaking engagement during which she apparently was focusing on the sinfulness of mankind and the need for God's grace. Spontaneously, Florence asked, "Does anyone here know what grace means?" A 7-year-old girl on the front row, all decked out in a white dress, stood up and raised her hand. "I know, Miss Littauer, I know," she said. "Grace is unmerited favor from God!"

Florence couldn't believe what she had just heard. She then asked the young girl to step up to the platform with her. "Great answer," Florence said, "now tell the audience what that means."

The little girl folded her hands and shrugged, "I don't have a clue!"

I've laughed about that incident every time I think about it, yet I am concerned about those who truly don't have a clue about God's grace and what it means. Mark Twain once said, "Heaven goes by favor. If it went by merit, you would step out and your dog would go in."

In II Corinthians 6:1, 2, Paul says, *"As God's fellow workers, we urge you not to receive God's grace in vain. For he says, 'In the time of my favor I heard you, and in the day of salvation I helped you.' I tell you, now is the time of God's favor, now is the day of salvation."*

These words rolled through my mind recently as I pulled my rental car onto Billy Graham Parkway in Charlotte, North Carolina. How often I have heard Billy Graham say, "This is your hour of decision, this is your moment of truth!" And he is so right! We live in the day of God's grace. *"For the grace of God that brings salvation has appeared to all men" (Titus 2:11).* We live in a time of God's favor.

Maybe if you are being totally honest like the little girl, you are saying, "What is grace?"

Grace is God Supplying Our Needs

Grace is not just a prayer we offer before meals. Nor is it just the name of a person that we have met along the way. Grace is God at work in our lives. D.L. Moody once said, "Grace is the act of God supplying our needs from day to day as we have them, found in the atonement of Christ." He shed his blood on Calvary's cruel cross to provide grace sufficient to cover all of our sins.

As a young teen attending the historic Mount of Praise camp meeting in Circleville, Ohio, I heard Dr. T.M. Anderson tell of the famed British preacher, Charles Spurgeon, riding home after a hard day's work, feeling tired and depressed. Suddenly, the promise "My grace is sufficient for you" entered his mind. He thought of the tiny fish who might be afraid lest they drink the river dry, but who hear the reassuring word, "Drink up little fish, my stream is sufficient for you." Spurgeon also thought of a mountain climber who is afraid he might exhaust all of the thin oxygen in the atmosphere. "Breathe away, young man, and fill your lungs," God says, "for my atmosphere is sufficient for you." Spurgeon said that for the first time, he "experienced the joy that Abraham felt when he rejoiced in God's provision."

> *"God has not promised to give us all the answers,*
> *but He has promised Grace!"*[1]
> *Barbara Johnson*

At a Billy Graham crusade, the late Corrie ten Boom told the story of how as a child she went to her father and said: "Papa, I don't think I have the faith to handle real trouble. I don't know what I'd do if you should die. I don't think I have the faith that some people have to face trouble."

Corrie's father looked at her tenderly and said, "Corrie, dear, when your father says he will send you to the store tomorrow, does he give the money to you today? No, he gives it to you when you are ready to go to the store. And if you are going on a train trip and need money for a ticket, does your father give you the money when we decide you may take the trip? No. He gives it to you when you are at the depot, all ready to buy your ticket. Corrie, God treats us the same way. He doesn't give you faith until you have a need. When you do, He will certainly give it to you."

The title of this book, *God Has Never Failed Me...But He Sure Has Scared Me to Death a Few Times* became an every day reality when I accepted my first full–time ministerial assignment in 1973.

Moving to Tampa, Florida, to become a young church planter with my new bride, Linda, was indeed an exercise in faith! We drove our car from the college campus to Florida by faith. Eating lots of Hamburger Helper became a way of life! We simply learned to rely on the grace of God to meet our every need. On one occasion, I felt led by the Lord to send $50 to the Carters, missionaries to the American Indians in Arizona, even though I wasn't sure why. Linda and I examined our checkbook and found just $54! Well, we sent the $50 anyhow and the next day, I went back to the post office. To my surprise, my college roommate, J. Michael Walters, had sent us a letter and enclosed a love gift of $50! (Pretty amazing, considering that he was a student at Asbury Seminary.) Naturally, I hurried home to share the good news with Linda. On the way home, I began to sing an old hymn...

"*Tis so sweet to trust in Jesus,*

Just to take Him at His Word,

Just to rest upon His promise.

Just to know: 'Thus saith the Lord.'

Jesus, Jesus, how I trust Him!

How I've proved Him o'er and o'er!

*Jesus, Jesus, precious Jesus! O **for***

***grace** to trust Him more!*[2]

Obviously, we were satisfied that God had met our need overnight! But the Carters wrote back two weeks later and said, "Your check for $50 arrived just on time. We were preparing to cancel a doctor's appointment for our daughter, Angie, because we didn't have the money." Would you believe, they needed exactly $50!

In his book, *The Applause of Heaven*, Max Lucado gives a magnificent portrait of God. Following his declaration that God does not save us because of what we've done, he adds these provocative words: "Only a puny god could be bought with tithes. Only an egotistical god would be impressed with our pain. Only a temperamental god could be satisfied by sacrifices. Only a heartless god would sell salvation to the highest bidders. And only a great God does for his children what they can't do for themselves."

He then adds this poignant description of God's grace: "God's delight is received upon surrender, not awarded upon conquest. The first step to joy is a plea for help."[3]

No wonder the Apostle Paul said, "*But he said to me, 'My grace is sufficient for you, for my power is made perfect in weakness. Therefore, I will boast all the more gladly about my weaknesses so that Christ's power may rest on me. That is why I delight in weaknesses, in insults, in hardships, in persecutions, in difficulties. For when I am weak, then I am strong.*" 2 Corinthians 12:9. God hears our plea for help and provides sufficient grace. And He is never late.

Grace Is God Cleansing Us From Sin

"*For it is by grace you have been saved through faith, and this not from yourselves. It is the gift of God — not by works, so that no one* can boast." Ephesians 2:8, 9 is a wonderful passage of scripture; in fact, almost all evangelical Christians exult in the fact that salvation is by grace through faith and is not based on works or merit on our part. We turned in faith to Jesus Christ alone for our salvation.

Milton Cunningham, a missionary, illustrates this truth so wonderfully. Milton was flying on a plane from Atlanta to Dallas recently. When he sat down on the plane, he happened to have the middle of the three seats on one side of the aisle. To his right, sitting next to the window, was a young girl who obviously had Down's Syndrome. This young girl began to ask him some very simple but almost offensive questions.

"Mister," she said to Cunningham, "did you brush your teeth this morning?"

Cunningham, very shocked at the question, squirmed around a bit and then said, "Well, yes, I brushed my teeth this morning."

The young girl said, "Good, 'cause that's what you're supposed to do." Then she asked, "Mister, do you smoke?"

Again, Cunningham was a little uncomfortable, but he told her with a little chuckle, no, he didn't.

She said, "Good, 'cause smoking will make you die." Then she said, "Mister, do you love Jesus?"

Cunningham was really caught by the simplicity and the forthrightness of her questions. He smiled and said, "Well, yes, I do love Jesus."

The little girl with Down's Syndrome smiled and said, "Good, 'cause we're all supposed to love Jesus."

About that time, just before the plane was ready to leave, another man came and sat down on the aisle seat next to Cunningham and began to read a magazine. The little girl nudged Cunningham again and said, "Mister, ask him if he brushed his teeth this morning."

Cunningham was really uneasy with that one, and said that he didn't want to do it. But she kept nudging him and saying, "Ask him! Ask him!" So Cunningham turned to the man seated next to him and said, "Mister, I don't mean to bother you, but my friend here wants me to ask you if you brushed your teeth this morning."

The man looked startled, of course. But when he looked past Cunningham and saw the young girl sitting there, he could tell her good intentions, so he took her question in stride and said with a smile, "Well, yes, I brushed my teeth this morning."

As the plane taxied onto the runway and began to take off, the young girl nudged Cunningham once more and said, "Ask him if he smokes." And so, good–naturedly, Cunningham did, and the man said that he didn't smoke.

As the plane was lifting into the air, the little girl nudged Cunningham once again and said, "Ask him if he loves Jesus."

Cunningham said, "I can't do that. That's too personal. I don't feel comfortable saying that to him."

But the girl smiled and insisted, "Ask him! Ask him!"

Cunningham turned to the fellow one more time and said, "Now she wants to know if you love Jesus."

The man could have responded like he had to the two previous questions — with a smile on his face and a little chuckle in his voice. And he almost did, but then the smile on his face disappeared, and his expression became serious. Finally he said to Cunningham, "You know, in all honesty, I can't say that I do. It's not that I don't want to, it's just that I don't know Him. I don't know how to know Him. I've wanted to be a person of faith all my life, but I haven't known how to do it. And now I've come to a time in my life when I really need that very much."

As the plane soared through the skies between Atlanta and Dallas, Milton Cunningham listened to the fellow talk about the brokenness in his life and shared his own personal story and testimony. He explained how to become a person of faith. He did that all because a little girl with Down's Syndrome asked him to ask the fundamental question that all Christians should be finding a way to communicate, "Do you love Jesus?"

I was never so aware of the need to communicate my faith until I was a senior in college. The phone rang in my college dorm with the news that my Uncle J.C. had died an alcoholic's death on skid row in Chicago, Illinois, and the family wanted me to do the funeral. I breathed a prayer that God would use me to be a witness to unsaved loved ones, packed my bags and loaded them and all the family into Dad's Buick and headed for Chicago.

I hadn't been in the city 45 minutes when God began to answer my prayers. Mom, Dad, Grandma Brewster, Terry, Richie, and I went downtown to the cemetery office to purchase a plot for Uncle J.C. Terry and I remained in the car with Richie, Uncle J.C.'s drinking pal. Richie looked at me and said, "You're a preacher, aren't you?"

"Yes," I replied, "I am a preacher. Why do you ask?"

He said, "I've been praying that God would send me a preacher. Preacher, I don't want to be lost like J.C. I want to go to heaven. Can you help me?"

Carefully and tenderly I began to share that receiving Jesus Christ is as simple as ABC.

A – Admit that you have sinned. And I read these words, "*For all have sinned and fall short of the glory of God*" Romans 3:23. Richie had no problem with that verse. He said, "I'm undesirable, unmentionable, and totally undone without God or His Son! I'm a dirty rotten sinner!"

Then I shared *B* – Believe that Jesus Christ can save you. "*Yet to all who received him, to those who believed in his name, he gave the right to become children of God*" John 1:12.

Finally, *C* – Confess Him as Lord of your life. "*That if you confess with your mouth, 'Jesus is Lord,' and believe in your heart that God raised him from the dead, you will be saved*" Romans 10:9. "Richie," I said, "are you willing to meet Christ on these terms?"

"I am," he said.

"Then let's pray." I began to lead him in prayer, and he repeated with me the following words: "Dear Lord Jesus, I know I'm a sinner. I believe that you died for my sins and arose from the grave. I now turn from my sins and invite you to come into my heart and life. I receive you as my personal Savior and follow you as my Lord." With the presence of God real and tears splashing down his cheeks and onto the rubber floormats in Daddy's Buick, Richie accepted Christ. He was in a moment dramatically changed from undesirable and undone to accepted and esteemed in the family of God!

About that time my mom, dad, and grandma came out and got into the front seat of the car. I explained to them that Richie had been saved, and if you have ever been to a camp meeting, you'll understand what happened next. My grandmother started shouting, and the next thing I knew my mother had joined in with praises to God. As we returned to Grandma's home, everyone shared their excitement about Richie's acceptance of Christ. Then it happened. Richie reached into his pocket and pulled out a Lucky Strike cigarette. The way I was raised, Christians didn't smoke, but *nobody* smoked in Daddy's Buick. I was stunned! He had just been saved and now he was smoking a cigarette. After Richie had nearly finished smoking the first cigarette, he turned to me and said, "I have a question for you, preacher. Now that I have accepted Jesus, is it right or wrong for me to smoke cigarettes?"

Well, that created a difficult situation, because I had to think about the potential of discouraging my new convert. "Richie," I said, "you know it could hurt your Christian witness." Unimpressed, he reached in and took out another cigarette and lit it. Now, there were some doubters in Daddy's Buick! The shouting had subsided.

"Preacher," he said, "I asked you a question. Is it right or wrong to smoke, now that I have accepted Christ?"

Well, I had a spark of inspiration because the Surgeon General had just come out with that warning on the back of the cigarette packs that cigarettes cause lung cancer. So I said to Richie, "Let me see your cigarette pack." I began to read from the back of his Lucky Strike pack that the Surgeon General had clearly stated that cigarettes could cause cancer. He was not impressed! For the third time, Richie took out a cigarette (obviously a chain smoker!)

He looked at me and said, "Preacher, I asked you a question. For the third time, is it right or wrong for me to smoke now that I have accepted Christ?"

Instantly, I began restating my position on smoking. "Richie," I replied, "First of all, it's not good for your witness; secondly, remember the Surgeon General said it is not good for your health." Suddenly, I had a moment of brilliance. "Richie," I said, "In my college class last week, my professor told us about Dr. Charles Hadden Spurgeon, pastor of the great Metropolitan Baptist Tabernacle, the prince of preachers. Believe it or not, he was a smoker. But one day, he traveled downtown to the tobacco shop. To his surprise and amazement, the display case at the tobacco shop contained an advertisement with the type of tobacco Dr. Spurgeon smoked. When Spurgeon saw it on display, he said, 'I'll have no part of that. I'll quit smoking before I influence people in the wrong manner!' Richie was not moved. "Doesn't it say somewhere in the Bible that we are to cleanse ourselves from all filthiness of flesh and spirit, perfecting holiness in the fear of God?"

"Yes, sir," I said, "it does!"

Richie said, "That's good enough for me. I quit!" With a sense of finality he crushed the last cigarette in the ash tray. Everyone in Daddy's Buick breathed a sigh of relief!

Several years later I was to return to Chicago to conduct the funeral of my Aunt Shirley. I remember breathing the same prayer, "God, use me to be a witness to my unsaved loved ones."

After arriving in Chicago, I went straight to the funeral home. My Grandma Brewster hugged me and introduced me to Richie's mother. "How's Richie doing?" I asked.

"Great," she replied. "He moved to Kentucky, got back with his wife and children. And, Preacher, you'll never believe it. Richie not only has quit drinking, he hasn't smoked since your Uncle J.C. passed away!"

Yes, here was a man who had been living on Chicago's Skid Row selling his blood to buy cheap wine, "undesirable and totally undone," praying that God would send him a preacher...and God sent him one at just the right moment. God is never late when you need grace!

A story I heard my mother share often as a child in Children's Church beautifully illustrates what happened in Richie's life.

A little boy had been taught by his father how to carve toys out of driftwood. The boy's greatest accomplishment was making a boat, complete with sails, rigging and rudder. The day came for him to test the water–worthiness of his boat. With great joy, he placed the boat in the water and watched it drift away, as the breeze filled the sails. Suddenly, a strong gust of wind came up and broke the twine attached to the boat, and with no one around to help, he tearfully watched his prize boat sail out of reach and out of sight.

Days went by. One day as he approached a store where various toy boats were sold, he thought he saw his boat in the window. Realizing that it *was* his boat, he went in to identify it as his own creation. The shop owner told him that he would have to buy his boat back. Retreating, he counted his money and decided to purchase his boat. As the little guy walked out of the shop, he was heard to say, "You are my boat twice over. I made you and now I have bought you."

Never forget God made you and He wants to save you! Remember the words of this old hymn:

Amazing grace! How sweet the sound

that saved a wretch like me!

I once was lost, but now am found;

Was blind, but now I see.[4]

[1]Barbara Johnson, *Mama, Get the Hammer! There's a Fly On Papa's Head* (Dallas: Word Publishing, 1994), p. 172.

[2]Louisa M.R. Stead (Words: 1882), William J. Kirkpatrick (Music: 1882), "'Tis So Sweet to Trust in Jesus" (Public Domain).

[3]Max Lucado, *The Applause of Heaven* (Dallas: Word Publishing, 1990), pp. 32, 33.

[4]John Newton (Words: 1779), Virginia Harmony (Music: 1831), "Amazing Grace" (Public Domain).

3

Coping With Life When You Can't Even Program Your VCR

M any people are doomed by what one might call a "Charlie Brown complex." Poor Charlie Brown can't do anything right. Of course, Lucy doesn't help. "You, Charlie Brown, are a foul ball in the line drive of life!" she often says.

Loud and clear!

Recently, I came across this list in my files:

You know it's going to be a bad day when:

1. *You turn on the morning news, and they're showing emergency routes out of your city.*
2. *The sun comes up in the west.*
3. *Your boss tells you not to bother taking off your coat.*
4. *You jump out of bed in the morning, and you miss the floor.*
5. *The bird singing outside your bedroom window is a buzzard.*
6. *You wake up in the morning, and your dentures are locked together.*
7. *Your horn accidentally gets stuck, and you're following a group of Hell's Angels on the freeway.*
8. *You put both contact lenses in the same eye.*

9. *You walk to work on a summer morning and find the bottom of your dress is tucked into the back of your panty hose.*

10. *You call your answering service, and they tell you it's none of your business.*

11. *Your income tax check bounces.*

12. *You put your bra or your athletic supporter on backwards and it fits better.*

13. *You step on your scale and it flashes, "Tilt, Tilt, Tilt."*

14. *The Suicide Prevention Hotline puts you on hold.*

15. *As the moving van starts to unload next door, the first four items down the ramp are dirt bikes.*

16. *Your pacemaker is recalled by the manufacturer.*

17. *Your church treasurer says, "The IRS called about some of your donations."*

Source Unknown

It was late Sunday evening, and what a full day it had been. I had preached twice, visited the hospital on an emergency call, and conducted a special board meeting concerning our building program. The moment I entered the church parsonage, the phone rang. I loosened my necktie, sat down at the hallway phone table and answered with the weary voice of a tired pastor.

To my chagrin, it was Sister Bertha Betterthanyou, and she had been talking to Brother Walkthehalls. She was just calling to register a complaint that many people in the church were upset with the new building program. For the next 30 minutes she took me to task on every facet of ministry. What a nightmare!

Her voice was so shrill and so loud that I laid the phone down, and I could still hear her as she continued to hammer me.

Upstairs, my wife was giving our 18-month-old son, Seth, his evening bath. Bathing Seth was often a challenge; he loved to escape from the bathtub when his mother was not looking and this night was no exception. As Sister Bertha droned on, I heard the saintly voice of Linda yelling, "Seth Aaron Toler, come back here!" (All mothers mean business when they use the child's middle name!)

Startled, I looked up and discovered Seth sliding down the stairs head first, naked and yelling for me at the top of his voice. He stood up quickly and headed for me. Undaunted by the noise in the background, Sister Bertha kept on talking. By this time, Seth was climbing into my lap soaking wet. He shivered and shook his curly blond head and water covered my blue Sunday suit. But he wasn't finished. He gave me a somewhat toothless grin, hugged me, and kissed me on each cheek. "Daddy," he said, "I wuv you!" His mother, not far behind, caught up! She wrapped him in a bath towel and off they went to complete his bath, oblivious to the fact that I had been in great need of a hug!

Tears streamed down my cheeks, and the frown that creased my face turned to a smile as Sister Bertha finalized her Sunday evening "fireside" chat with me. In that moment, only one thing mattered. I knew I was loved. God was not late when I needed encouragement!

Perhaps you have heard the story of the fellow who was about to jump from a bridge. An alert police officer slowly, methodically moved toward him, talking with him all the time.

When he got within inches of the man, he said, "Surely nothing could be bad enough for you to take your life. Tell me about it. Talk to me."

The would–be jumper told how his wife had left him, how his business had become bankrupt, how his friends had deserted him. Everything in life had lost meaning. For 30 minutes he told the sad story. Then they both jumped!

I love the Far Side cartoon series. A recent cartoon pictured two cowboys out on the range and illustrates how contagious discouragement can be. One cowboy says to the other, "The buffalo is the ugliest animal in the world." Nearby a buffalo is heard to say, "I think I've just heard a discouraging word!"

We all suffer with bouts of discouragement. Haven't you? Are you suffering from discouragement? It may be a relationship that's gone south, a job that's been lost, or the death of a loved one. Without doubt, negative people and negative circumstances can combine to stifle our spiritual lives.

Alexandra Kropotkin, in an article titled, "Homemade," described the death of her friend. "One day a millionaire of my acquaintance, whose pride it was never to offer a tip for any service, faced an unforgettable tragedy. His chief accountant committed suicide. The books were found to be in perfect order; the affairs of the dead man, a modest bachelor, were prosperous and calm. The only letter left by the accountant was a brief note to his millionaire employer. It read: "In 30 years I have never had one word of encouragement. I'm fed up."[1]

"Discouragement comes when you try to start with
what you wish you had but don't have. And it intensifies

when you insist on trying to be in a position you are not in
and probably never will be in."[2]
Stuart Briscoe

During the Boer War (1899 – 1902), a man was convicted of a very unusual crime: being a "discourager." The South African town of Ladysmith had been under attack, and this traitor had moved up and down the lines of soldiers who were defending the city and did everything he could to discourage them. He pointed out the enemy's strength, the difficulty of defending against them, and the inevitable capture of the city. He hadn't used a gun in his attack. It hadn't been necessary. His weapon had been the power of discouragement.

Encouragement, on the other hand, can be a powerful friend. It strengthens the weak, imparts courage to the fainthearted, and gives hope to the faltering.

The Apostle Paul gives us four ways to handle any discouragement we might experience in life. The following scripture verse offers a fool–proof formula for overcoming discouragement: *"Therefore, since through God's mercy we have this ministry, we do not lose heart"* 2 Corinthians 4:1.

The Mercy of God

In 1984, I was privileged to travel around the world for World Relief Corporation and World Gospel Mission, visiting refugee camps, and speaking to and encouraging mission leaders on matters of leadership, church growth, and evangelism. I also visited many of the great growing churches of the world. Upon arrival in Seoul, Korea, Linda and I and our dear friends, David and Mary Vaughn, caught a taxi and headed to the Full Gospel Central Church. A mutual friend, Dr. Holland London, Sr. had made special arrangements for us to visit Dr. David (Paul) Cho's office and church. Dr. Cho's administrative assistant, Miss Lee, gave us a tour of the huge 25,000-seat sanctuary and the additional education units on the church property.

It was especially exhilarating to observe 2,000 people in line on Tuesday afternoon waiting to be baptized! Miss Lee informed us that this was an every day occurrence and a direct answer to the prayers of God's people. We were greatly moved by the phenomenal growth of the great church under the leadership of Dr. Cho. Later, we attended the Sunday services. Dr. Cho told of how the church began with a small tent and five people. As he continued to reflect on the history of this great church, he said, "I became so discouraged in 1969 when we were building the new sanctuary that I went to the 18th floor of the educational building and contemplated jumping out!"

Unbelievable! This man who pastors the largest church in the world (last count was 500,000 members) became so discouraged that he felt like ending his life! But God was faithful. Dr. Cho said, "God came to my rescue. Just in the midst of my discouragement He brought peace and encouragement!"

The Comfort of God and Friends

The Apostle Paul, who had been stoned, shipwrecked, beaten, snake–bitten and spat upon, had the first answer to discouragement. *"Through God's mercy, though we are wasting away, yet inwardly we are being renewed day by day. For our light and momentary troubles are achieving for us an eternal glory that far outweighs them all"* 2 Corinthians 4:16. *"But God, who comforts the downcast, comforted us by the coming of Titus"* 2 Corinthians

7:6. Apparently, Paul was somewhat frightened about the future. He realized that life was passing by quickly "wasting away", but he found comfort from God and Titus. God always has someone to speak words of comfort when you are literally scared to death. God has never failed to bring comfort during my darkest hours.

There was a time early in my ministry when I was going to quit! I was so discouraged, that I began reading the classified ads in the newspaper, looking for a new career. In the midst of my discouragement, my mother came to town to spend the weekend. On Friday evening with tear–filled eyes, I told Mother that I was going to leave the ministry. Instantly, she got out of her La–Z–Boy rocker, walked over to me, placed her hands on my head and began to pray, "God, you called my son into the ministry, you anointed him to preach the gospel. Tell the devil to take his hands off my son, and God, encourage Stanley right now." Let me tell you, a new determination and energy flowed immediately through my inner being. God brought comfort through my dear mother — the only person to ever call me Stanley.

Pastor and theologian Richard Niebuhr was teaching a class. Near the end of the lecture he said, "Whatever comes into our lives, God can turn around for good." In that same class was a student who, just a few weeks before, had been involved in a boating accident. The student had lost his mother and father, his only sibling, and his fiancee. He alone had survived. There were those in the class who thought Dr. Niebuhr was either crazy or simply insensitive to the events of the past weeks.

The lecture ended, and all the students stayed, expecting to see the grieving young man angrily accuse the professor of making such an insensitive theological statement. But what happened surprised them all. The student walked up to Dr. Niebhur, shook his hand, and said, "Thank you, sir. That is the only thing that makes life worthwhile." He then turned and walked away.

It is true. God is good. But that does not mean that bad things will not happen. Floods come, the earth quakes, people die, and marriages break up. We cry, but so does God. Remember the powerful words of Isaiah 53:4, as he foretold the coming of the Messiah: *"Surely he has borne our griefs and carried our sorrows."* When we hurt, God cares. When we are in pain, God is present to comfort. When alone, God can be a strengthening companion.

If you need comfort this very moment, consider the words of the old hymn, "God Will Take Care of You":

> (Verse 1)
>> *Be not dismayed what e're betide.*
>> *God will take care of you.*
>> *Beneath His wings of love abide.*
>> *God will take care of you.*
>
> (Verse 4)
>> *No matter what will be the test,*
>> *God will take care of you.*
>> *Lean, weary one, upon His breast.*
>> *God will take care of you.*
>
> (Chorus)
>> *God will take care of you.*
>> *Thro' ev'ry day, o'er all the way.*
>> *He will take care of you;*
>> *God will take care of you.*[3]

Dietrich Bonhoeffer in his book, *The Cost of Discipleship*, noted "Christians have forgotten the ministry of listening that has been committed to them by the One who is Himself the great listener." Certainly, this great scholar challenges every believer to improve his or her listening skills.

After reading Bonhoeffer's book, I began to implement the following methods as a part of my encouragement ministry.

1. **Writing letters**. Several years ago, I read an article in *Guideposts* magazine entitled, "The Power of A Note," written by Norman Vincent Peale. It challenged Christians to write "short, spontaneous, specific notes of encouragement." Since reading Peale's article, I have practiced this ritual of comfort, and I might add that I have the worst handwriting in the world! Recently, I wrote a note of encouragement to a friend who claims he took it to the local pharmacist to be deciphered. They gave him a prescription for Valium! So, even if he couldn't read my note, he got a great laugh at my expense!

Talk show host Larry King reported that during his hospital stay he had many letters and gifts. King mentioned on his TV show that the letter that touched him the most was the one sent by Pete Maravich, former NBA star. Pete included a Bible and the following note: "Dear Larry, I'm so glad to hear that everything went well with your surgery. I want you to know that God was watching over you every minute, and even though I know you may question that, I also know that one day it will be revealed to you...because He lives."

One week later, King noted, Pete Maravich, college basketball and NBA luminary, died.

Pastor Greg Asimakoupoulos states, "I keep a handy file folder of short notes and cards from individuals in my desk drawer. These notes provide a quick resource of encouragement when doubt or congregational turmoil bring discouragement." After hearing this, I began the same practice. What a lift it can bring on a dark, cloudy day!

2. **Compassionate listening.** In a book entitled, *The Power of Encouragement*, the author Jean Doering tells about a little girl who went to comfort the mother of a playmate who had recently died. When she returned home, her mother asked what she had done to comfort the mother of her playmate. She said, "I just climbed up in her lap and cried with her." Ask God to give you a compassionate heart!

3. **The touch of the hand.** The day had finally arrived. Eighty–two–year–old Dr. Paul S. Rees, great expositor and ministry statesman, was speaking at the annual ministerial convention. Dr. Rees was a model preacher for me. I had listened to his tapes, read his books, and was finally getting the chance to meet him! I was more than a little excited. We had named our newborn son, Seth, after Dr. Rees' father, Seth Cook Rees.

The break time was my chance to greet Dr. Rees. After waiting in line for 15 minutes, my turn came. I shook hands with him and told him about our new son, Seth. Dr. Rees asked, "Do you have a picture of your son?" As any proud father, I instantly produced a photo of my son. "What a good-looking little guy!" Dr. Rees said. "Would it be OK if I prayed for him?"

"Of course," I replied, "please do so!" Dr. Rees proceeded to place his hand over the picture of Seth in my outstretched hand

and prayed a brief but sensitive prayer. I cried like a baby, and so did other ministers waiting in the same line.

When I returned home from the convention, I shared with Linda what had taken place. We wept together in appreciation for the prayer of blessing by Dr. Rees. After experiencing the prayerful touch from the hand of Dr. Paul S. Rees, I decided that I would take parishioners by the hand and pray with them as they shared with me their joys and sorrows. There is power in the touch for us. Martin Luther once said, "We are all little Christs — when we touch, He touches."

Several years ago on the campus of Southern Nazarene University, where I currently serve as Pastor–in–Residence, a conference for ministers was held. One of the speakers, Dr. Morris Weigelt, shared about a time of deep depression in his life. I was especially touched when he talked about a night during his hospitalization. Morris told the group of ministers that during the middle of the night "all of his insecurities and depression came upon him."

Weigelt got out of bed and walked the halls looking for someone awake and willing to give him a hug. With a great deal of pathos and humor, he concluded that all he could find was a huge, burly security guard. "Sir," he said, "Would you give me a hug?"

"I sure will!" the security guard responded. Dr. Weigelt indicated that he found comfort and encouragement from the touch of the big burly security guard. He returned to his room and slept peacefully.

> *Lord, make me an instrument of Thy peace.*
> *Where there is hatred, let me sow love;*
> *Where there is injury, pardon;*

Where there is doubt, faith;
Where there is despair, hope;
Where there is darkness, light;
Where there is sadness, joy;
O Divine Master, grant that I may
not so much seek to be consoled, as console;
to be understood, as to understand;
to be loved as to love.
For it is in giving, that we receive;
It is in pardoning, that we are pardoned;
It is in dying, that we are born to eternal life.
Amen.
St. Francis of Assisi

Confidence in Our Future With Christ

Paul said in II Corinthians 5:5, *"Now it is God who has made us for this very purpose and has given us the Spirit as a deposit, guaranteeing what is to come."*

My friend, Talmadge Johnson, told the story of the man who stopped to watch a Little League baseball game. He asked one of the youngsters what the score was. "We're losing 18-0," was the answer.

"Well," said the man, "I must say you don't look discouraged."

"Discouraged?" the boy said, puzzled. "Why should we be discouraged? We haven't come to bat yet."

The Courage to Take a Giant Step of Faith

You have the power of choice! You can choose to be discouraged, depressed, and live life in a dark, dingy dungeon. Or you can go out on a limb with God and make a commitment to move forward with God.

In his lectures, Carl Sandburg often included the story of 7–year–old Abe Lincoln. One evening, Abe walked over to his cabin door and opened it. He looked up into the face of the full moon and said, "Mr. Moon, what do you see from way up there?"

Mr. Moon answered, "Abe, I see a calendar and it says 1816. I see eight million people in the United States of America. I see 16,000 covered wagons plodding slowly across the midwestern plains toward California. And, Abe, I see far to the west a wagon in the desert between two ridges of the Rocky Mountains. The wagon is broken, weeds are crawling in the spokes and there is an old dusty skeleton nearby with a pair of empty moccasins and some dry bones. I also see a sign that says, The cowards never started!

Why not rely on the promises of God and choose to be encouraged rather than discouraged?

This Christmas season they are advertising a VCR on television with the guarantee that "*anyone* can program it!" Admittedly, I'm skeptical. I've never yet been able to figure out our VCR! But one thing I am sure about: if God says it in His Word, that settles it for me! My encouragement is not in the guarantees and empty promises of this world! It is in my future with Christ!

> "*How great is the love the Father has lavished on us, that we should be called children of God! And that is what we are! The reason the world does not know us is that it did not know him. Dear friends, now we are children of God, and what we will be has not yet been made known. But we know that when*

he appears, we shall be like him, for we shall see him as he is. Everyone who has this hope in him purifies himself, just as he is pure" I John 3:1-3.

[1]Alexandra Kropotkin, *"Homemade"*, ISSN 0899–5494 (Vol. 15, No. 1, January 1991).

[2]Stuart Briscoe, *Bound for Joy*, (Regal Books 1975, 1984), p. 95.

[3]Civilla D. Martin (Words: 1904), W. Sullivan Martin (Music: 1904), "God Will Take Care of You" (Public Domain).

4

*All May Be Fair in Love and War,
But Not Much in Life Is!*

My long–time friend, Chuck Crow, loves to tell the story of the old man who is dying as his wife of more than 50 years is seated beside his bed. Fred opens his eyes and sees Martha. "There you are, Martha," he said, "at my side once again."

"Yes, dear," Martha said.

"In retrospect," the old man said, "I remember all the times that you've been at my side. You were there when I was drafted and had to go off to fight in the Korean War. You were there with me when our first house burned to the ground. And you were there when I had the accident that destroyed our little Volkswagen. Yes, you were there when our little shoe shop went belly–up and I lost every cent I had."

"Yes, honey," his wife said.

Fred sighed deeply. "I tell you, Martha," he said, "You're bad luck!"

It is difficult to find a more basic problem than our confusion about human relations. Not long ago I attended a marriage seminar taught by widely known counselor, Norman Wright. Dr.

Wright pointed out two basic reasons that relationships fail: *fear*, which causes us to erect barriers; and *selfishness*, which causes us to focus on fulfilling our own needs instead of the needs of others.

Dr. Wright also discussed three vital qualities that enable us to develop lasting relationships: *genuineness*, which enables us to be who we are without a facade; *nonpossessive love*, which enables us to accept a person as he or she is and allow him space; and *empathy*, which enables us to feel with another person.[1]

Paula Schmed, in an article titled, *"Ever Had An Achy Breaky Heart?"* said that smash hit by Billy Ray Cyrus was just one of the more recent country music songs to put into words the woeful feelings of a love gone bad.

But country music has been doing that for decades. Check out some of these country–fied lost–love lines passed down through the years:

"Flushed from the bathroom of your heart" — Jack Clement 1967

"I only miss you on days that end in 'Y'" — Jim Malloy, 1975

"How come your dog don't bite nobody but me?" — *Wayne Walker and Mel Tillis, 1961*

"My tears have washed 'I love you' from the blackboard of my heart" — Hank Thompson and Lyle Gaston, 1956

But it ain't all bad news. Some of country's love songs are quite - well - uplifting. Wouldn't you just love to hear your date say:

"Old King Kong was just a little monkey compared to my love for you" — Sammy Lyons, 1977

"If I don't love you, grits ain't groceries" — George Jones, 1959

Had enough? If not, check out the book *"I've Got Tears in My Ears from Lyin' on My Back in My Bed While I Cry Over You"* — *Country Music's Best (and Funniest) Lines.*[1]

In pre–marital counseling over the years I have frequently shared the stages of a marriage through the description of a husband's reactions over a 7–year period to his wife's cold:

1st Year: Sugar dumpling, I'm worried about you, baby girl. You've got a bad sniffle. I'm putting you in the hospital for a general check–up.

2nd Year: Listen, honey, go to bed. I've called the doctor to rush over here.

3rd Year: Better lie down, nothing like a little rest when you feel bad. I'll bring you something to eat.

4th Year: Look dear, be sensible, after you feed the kids, and get the dishes washed, you'd better lie down for awhile.

5th Year: Why don't you get up and get yourself an aspirin? And stop complaining so much!

6th Year: If you'd just gargle or something instead of sitting around and barking in my face like a seal, I'd appreciate it.

7th Year: For Pete's sake, stop sneezing. What are you trying to do, give me pneumonia?!

(By the way, if you are laughing, your marriage may be going downhill, too!)

But it's not just marital relationships that are full of strife and strain. It's labor and management, and it is nations at war. Sadly, it seems as though every newscast carries a story about the inability of human beings to live in positive relationships with other human beings.

The phrase "you make me sick" is still frequently used in human relationships. I know it's only a phrase, but sometimes our emotions, in a challenging relationship, can actually affect our health.

Do people make you sick? Do you feel like life isn't fair when it comes to you and your relationships? Let me give you some very simple steps that will help you in your journey into good relationships.

Don't Curse People, Bless Them!

"Bless those who persecute you; bless and do not curse" Romans 12:14.

How much can one person bear? "More" would be the answer of Carson McCullers, the novelist who was described at her death as having a "vocation of pain."

"Much of her art," a critic related, "seemed to have flowed from her own tortured life."

Before she was 29, Mrs. McCullers had suffered three strokes that paralyzed her left side. Discouraged, she was sure that she could never write again. Eventually she resumed her work, writing a page a day.

However, her pain increased in her later years. Her husband committed suicide, and illness left her a virtual cripple. In a rare mention of her troubles, she said, "Sometimes I think God got me mixed up with Job. But Job never cursed God, and neither have I. I carry on."[3]

I like the story of one fellow who was bragging to some friends, "Yes, there is a proud fighting tradition in my family! My great–great–grandfather stood his ground at Bunker Hill. Then Great–Grandfather valiantly joined up with the troops to destroy the Germans. My grandfather was at Pearl Harbor. And my father fought the North Koreans—"

"Mercy!" one of his friends remarked. "Can't your family get along with anyone?"

Just this week I was watching "Good Morning, America", and Joan Lunden was interviewing the actress, Jamie Lee Curtis. Joan noted that many critics were surprised at her heavy use of profanity in her upcoming movie. Jamie responded, "I can curse like a sailor — a blue streak!" For certain, the world's way is to curse everything in sight. Not me. I want to bless everyone!

An Irish Prayer

May those who love us, love us;
And those that don't love us,
May God turn their hearts;
And if He doesn't turn their hearts,
May He turn their ankles
So we'll know them by their limping.

Love Everyone, Including Yourself

Loving God with your whole heart and understanding the love of God for you provides the foundation for loving yourself. All too often as Christians we fail to see the need to love ourselves and fall into the pit of self–degradation and false humility, resulting in poor self–esteem. It also causes a strain in many relationships.

Scripture clearly teaches that we are to love ourselves, or we cannot possibly love our neighbor.

> *Love is patient, love is kind. It does not envy, it does not boast, it is not proud. It is not rude, it is not self-seeking, it is not easily angered, it keeps no record of wrongs. Love does not delight in evil but rejoices with the truth. It always protects, always trusts, always hopes, always perseveres.*
>
> *Love never fails. But where there are prophecies, they will cease; where there are tongues, they will be stilled; where there is knowledge, it will pass away.*
>
> I Corinthians 13:4-8

I once heard Denis Waitley say, "The first best-kept secret of total success is that we feel love inside ourselves before we can give it to others." He went on to say, "If there is no sense of value within us, we have nothing to offer to others."

Romans 12:16 says, "*Live in harmony with one another.*" According to Jesus Christ, this is possible only "*when you love your neighbor as yourself.*"

IF YOU DON'T LOVE YOURSELF, YOU CAN'T POSSIBLY LOVE YOUR NEIGHBOR!

> *"Love is the medicine for the sickness of the world."*

A minister friend told me a story some time ago that illustrates beautifully the matter of self–worth in Christian experience. It seems a certain pastor had a very poor self–image.

He was the senior pastor, and things were not going well for him in his local church.

Feeling very discouraged, he entered the prayer chapel, knelt at the altar and prayed a very sad prayer. "O God, I am nothing. I am nothing," he said over and over again.

Just at that time, the associate pastor walked by and was very impressed by the senior pastor's humility. So he joined him in praying, "O Lord, I am nothing. I, too, am nothing."

While both were praying, the church custodian came by the prayer chapel and was moved by the apparent meekness of the leaders of the church. Not to be outdone, he joined them at the altar and said, "O Lord, I too, am nothing, nothing, nothing."

The associate pastor paused, looked at the custodian, then turned to the senior pastor and said, "Now look who thinks he's nothing."

Lee Iacocca once asked legendary football coach, Vince Lombardi, what it took to make a winning team. The book, *Iacocca,* records Lombardi's answer:

> "There are a lot of coaches with good ball clubs who know the fundamentals and have plenty of discipline but still don't win the game. Then you come to the third ingredient: If you're going to play together as a team, you've got to care for one another. You've got to love each other. Each player has to be thinking about the next guy and saying to himself: 'If I don't block that man, Paul is going to get his legs broken. I have to do my job well in order that he can do his.' The difference between mediocrity and greatness is the feeling these guys have for each other."[3]

My son, Seth, has always loved baseball. From the time he was 18 months old, he could swing a small bat and throw the ball. We would often watch the Cincinnati Reds play baseball on television and then go outside and play ball. Seth really loved to watch Johnny Bench hit home runs!

By the time he reached 4 years old, I became concerned about his knowledge of the game. Seth always "hit a home run" no matter where the ball went. I can still see him running around our imaginary infield, going into his "Pete Rose slide," taking off his hat, exposing his blond curly locks and looking up at the pitcher (me) and declaring, "Home run, Daddy!"

One afternoon we were in the front yard playing baseball. I decided it was time to teach Seth that we didn't always hit home runs! First, I launched into a significant lesson on what it means to make an "out." Then I began to explain the purpose of bases. Just about the time I had confused him thoroughly, his mother came out the front door with four of Seth's reading books. I got the idea — it didn't take a rocket scientist! — the books would serve as bases. Together we carefully placed the books at 1st, 2nd, 3rd base, and home plate. It was coming together. Then I explained to Seth, "If you overrun a base, and I tag you, you're out."

"OK, Daddy," he exclaimed, "play ball!"

I pitched a few balls and let Seth run the bases to warm up. Each time he went through the same ritual: head first slide into home plate, hat off, dust himself off, and the declaration of "Home run, Daddy!"

The big moment had arrived. I reviewed the rules with a warning: "Seth, if you overrun a base, I'll tag you out."

"OK, Daddy, play ball."

I reached back for my best pitch. Seth swung mightily and hit the ball toward short stop. I fielded it beautifully! (Remember, it's a one–man field.) He rounded first, his little legs churning. I called out, "I've got the ball. Don't overrun second base."

He kept going, and I tagged him just before he reached third base. "You're out!" I cried.

But Seth kept going. He rounded third and headed for home. Seth went into his patented slide at home plate, got up, took off his baseball cap, dusted his setter, sat down on home plate and said, "Home run, Daddy, home run!"

Arriving somewhat out of breath at the scene, I responded, "You're out!"

"Home run!" he said.

"You're out!" I retorted.

"Home run!" he yelled again.

"You're out!" I shot back.

Disgusted, he folded his chubby little arms, shook his curly head and said, "Daddy, it's my books, it's my ball, it's my bat, and if you don't play right, I'm going in the house!"

> *If you want to lose friends quickly,*
> *start bragging about yourself;*
> *if you want to make and keep friends,*
> *start bragging about others.*
>
> Anonymous

A survey by the Wisconsin Restaurant Association revealed why a restaurant's patrons stopped eating at a certain restaurant. The following reasons were cited:

1 percent   Died

3 percent   Moved away

5 percent   Developed other relationships

9 percent   Preferred a competitor

14 percent   Were dissatisfied about the product (meal)

68 percent   Felt an attitude of neglect or indifference [5]

"Do not be proud. But be willing to associate with people of low position" Romans 12:16. The writer continues in Romans 13:9 with an important reminder *"...and whatever other commandment there may be, are summed up in this one rule: Love your neighbor as yourself."*

> *"You have heard that it was said, 'Love your neighbor and hate your enemy.' But I tell you: Love your enemies and pray for those who persecute you, that you may be sons of your Father in heaven. He causes his sun to rise on the evil and the good, and sends rain on the righteous and the unrighteous."*
> Matthew 5:43-45

Harold Ivan Smith wrote one of my all-time favorite books, *The Jabez Principle.* In this insightful book, he says:

> *"My value comes in God's affirmation of me.*
> So if people reject me, I still have worth.
> So if my mate rejects me, I still have worth.
> So if my child rejects me, I still have worth.
> So if my employer rejects me, I still have worth.
> My worth is not in what I do or say
>   in what I acquire or own

in what I invent or create

It's in me — a unique person, created by God."[6]

Examine Your Motives

"Do not repay anyone evil for evil. Be careful to do what is right in the eyes of everybody" Romans 12:17. Now that's a real challenge! When others make you sick, you should ask the hard question, "Am I at fault? Do I frustrate people to the point of nausea?"

Someone has said, "Forgiveness is critical to a Christian's freedom because unforgiveness is the means Satan uses to gain ground in the life of the believer."

There are so many legends that surround the painting of "The Last Supper" by Leonardo da Vinci. One in particular gives us food for thought. It seems that just before the painting of the faces of the disciples in the portrayal of our Lord's last supper, da Vinci had a terrible argument with a fellow artist. He determined to paint his fellow artist's face into the portrait as that of Judas Iscariot, and thus take revenge by preserving the man in infamy and scorn to succeeding generations. Thus the face of Judas was one of the first he finished, and everyone could easily recognize the face of da Vinci's enemy.

However, when he came to paint the face of Christ he couldn't make any progress at all. Something seemed to be frustrating even his best efforts. He finally came to the conclusion that the cause of his difficulty was his bitterness toward his fellow painter. He decided that you cannot at the same time be painting the features of Christ into your own life and painting another with the colors of hatred and enmity.

Therefore, he chose to forgive in order to create!

Newspapers and television programs carried the story of Cindy Hartman in the summer of 1994. While living in Conway, Arkansas, Cindy's home was burglarized. It was at night, and Cindy was sleeping peacefully, unaware that a thief had entered her home. The phone rang, and as Cindy prepared to answer the phone, the burglar ripped the phone cord from the wall and ordered Cindy into her closet.

Cindy reported that she instantly fell to her knees and began crying out to God. During her prayer, she paused and asked the would–be thief if she could pray for him. In a state of disbelief, the burglar agreed to the prayer. Cindy began to tell God that she loved this man and forgave him for what he was doing to her.

Cindy Hartman related that the burglar fell to his knees and cried out to God for mercy and forgiveness. The burglar breathed a sigh of relief, got up and went to his car. He promptly unloaded everything he had taken from Cindy's home. Additionally, he unloaded the bullets from his gun and left it with Cindy.

Though frightened, Cindy chose to let God take care of the problem.

> *"It is well to remember that the entire population*
> *of the universe, with one trifling exception,*
> *is composed of others."*
> J.A. Holmes

Leave Revenge to God

"Do not take revenge my friends, and leave room for God's wrath. For it is written, it is mine to avenge. I will repay" Romans 12:19. That's right, give the person who makes you sick over to God!

I once had the marvelous privilege of hearing Victor Frankl speak. Frankl, a German/Jewish doctor who was arrested during World War II by the Gestapo, was placed in prison and thoroughly interrogated by the Nazi secret police under bright lights for hours at a time. They took every possession, even his wedding band! Frankl said, "I went through many senseless tortures from the hands of the Nazi policemen. I realized that I had only one thing left, the power to choose my own attitude, and I could choose bitterness or forgiveness."

He chose forgiveness! Victor Frankl stands as a wonderful example of leaving revenge to God.

Friend, leave revenge to God and in the sweet by and by, every knee will bow and every tongue confess. God will repay evil for evil!

> *"A drop of honey catches more flies than a gallon of gall."*
> *So with men. If you would win a man to your cause, first*
> *convince him that you are his sincere friend. Therein is a drop*
> *of honey which catches his heart, which, say what he will, is*
> *the high road to reason.*
>
> *Abraham Lincoln*

Surround Them With Love and Prayer

The ultimate test of your relationship with the Lord is when people treat you wrong, when they make you sick, you begin to pray for them.

"Dear God, help me to be willing to honestly look at my own life. God, help me to make changes that need to be made. God, help me to accept myself as you have accepted me. God, help me to give others the same spirit of love, friendship and opportunities that you have given me as your child. For I know as I give them love, friendship, and take every opportunity to bless them instead of curse them, your love has every potential of touching their lives and changing them for good. May I be your instrument in touching that person that makes me so sick. Today I surround them with love and prayers and believe that the end of the problem will be a healthy, loving, relationship with them."

[1]H. Norman Wright, *How To Get Along With Almost Anyone*, (Dallas: Word, 1989), pp. 15-24.

[2]Compiled by Paula Schwed (Andres and McMeel), *Campus Life*, October 1994, p. 39.

[3]A.D. Dennison, Jr., *Contemporary Illustrations for Speakers and Teachers*, (Grand Rapids: Zondervan Publishing 1976).

[4]Lee Iacocca with William Novak, *Iacocca*, (New York City: Bantam Books: 1984).

[5]George R. Walther, *Power Talking*, (New York: Berkley Books, 1991), p. 227.

[6]Harold Ivan Smith, *The Jabez Principle*, (Kansas City: Beacon Hill, 1989), pp. 116–117.

5

When the Going Gets Tough, the Tough Get Challenged

Tristan Blann, a 7-year-old cancer patient, always had three stops on Sunday morning at Nashville First Church.

His first stop was to visit "Mr. Frank," his Sunday school teacher (and supplier of candy). His next stop was to visit Uncle "Pek" Gunn, famous poet laureate of Tennessee and Tristan's supplier of bubble gum. His final stop was always to see me after the Sunday morning worship service. Invariably he would slap me in the center of the back while I was shaking hands with people, and I'd turn for him to leap into my arms. What a vigorous, enthusiastic, courageous little guy. With a shiny bald head and a million dollar smile, he'd say, "Hi Pastor!"

Tristan was the mascot for the 1991 Vanderbilt University basketball team, and you could find him perched on the bench at every game with head basketball coach, Eddie Folger. He was their No.1 cheerleader. He understood basketball and was a super little player. In and out of Vanderbilt University Hospital children's unit, Tristan would set up a goal in the courtyard and challenge any visitor to play. He loved to shoot hoops.

Perhaps his father, Dr. Rob Blann, described him best in this poem:

Shakespeare Would Have Liked My Son.
"Cowards die many times before their death
the valiant taste of death but once."
(Or at least that's what Shakespeare said).
But my son is valiant.
No one who knows him will deny that.
Yet he has tasted death many times.
He has lived on the poison that tries to kill his cancer.
My valiant son has lived for six more years
Because the doctors were able to poison the poison,
But now they say time has run out.
The chemo just can't work anymore.
One poison is just stronger than the other
And Tristan's many tastes of death
won't keep him much longer from the final one.
Shakespeare's right, you know.
I've just been playing with words
(like he was)
But if you're truly valiant, there is only one death:
so now I have nothing to do
but play with words
and wait for my son's last valiant act.

Rob Blann, October 29, 1991
Used with permission

On January 16, 1992, my 7-year-old friend, Tristan Blann, went to be with the Lord. Three days later, with the 1900-seat sanctuary of Nashville First Church the Nazarene full of friends and family, I preached his funeral. What an awesome worship service it was! The Vanderbilt University men's basketball team served as honorary pall bearers. Tributes were offered from around the country. Dale Brown, head coach of the Louisiana State Tigers, said, "The courage of Tristan Blann was amazing." Larry Woody, Sports Editor of *The Tennessean*, called Tristan "a valiant little warrior and a hero to his heroes." Tom Norman of the *Nashville Banner* said, "Tristan's positive attitude and courage during his illness were an inspiration to all."

This poem, written by Tristan's father, was read:

Midnight of Homecoming
When the house is at its darkest
and silence is so quiet that it screams
And I let myself leave the books to go to bed,
I pause at the children's door — his door actually,
and I watch them in their sleep.
I watch, midnight mad with the moon,
knowing that the little boy
won't be here in a year.
Bewildered with pain and lack of sleep
my mind keeps taking photographs
making memories of what won't be.
Tristan in the top bunk
Where I lifted him hours ago
After he had fallen asleep downstairs.
So happy with his homecoming
So exhausted after the harrowing hospital
And what they did to him there.
And then beautiful Jennifer
Lying there like a dream
Sleeping in his bottom bunk
forsaking her own room

Staying with him
Because he was afraid to be alone.
Oh God, stay with us when we are alone.

Rob Blann, September 19, 1991
Used with permission

Tears streamed down my cheeks. The words, "Oh, God, stay with us when we are alone," caused my mind to reflect back just 10 days earlier in Bethany, Oklahoma, standing in a cold, windy cemetery with friends Phil and Donna Moore grieving the loss of their beautiful 16-year-old daughter. Asthmatic, but otherwise healthy, Mandy had died unexpectantly. It all seemed so unfair to me. But just as Dr. Roger Hahn completed the benediction, I heard a beautiful tenor voice begin singing,

What a friend we have in Jesus,
All our sins and griefs to bear!

It was the voice of Mandy's father, Phil Moore. Hundreds joined in the singing:

What a privilege to carry everything to God in prayer!
O what peace we often forfeit,
O what needless pain we bear,
All because we do not carry everything to God in prayer.[1]

The words to the song soothed me as I pulled myself together to deliver the funeral message, with three important statements from Deuteronomy 33:23.

Only God Provides the Answers to Life

"*The eternal God is your refuge, and underneath are the everlasting arms. He will drive out the enemy before you saying, 'Destroy him'*" Deuteronomy 33:27. D.R. Davis in his book, *The*

World That We Have Forgotten, says, "Man in his quest for life is a creature of eternity." We are his creation! Solomon says in Ecclesiastes 3:11, *"He has made everything beautiful in its time. He has also set eternity in the hearts of men."*

Helen Keller, blind and deaf from infancy, became a noted writer and lecturer. At the age of nine, according to her biography, *The Miracle Worker,* her parents engaged a teacher to establish communication with her. The teacher, Anne Sullivan, took little Helen to the well one day and pumped cold water over her hand and then tapped on the palm of her hand. Helen miraculously began to learn communication skills. Often left untold is the fact that Helen Keller's parents were deeply devoted Christians who desperately wanted her to know about God. The Kellers contacted the great preacher, Phillips Brook and asked him to tutor Helen in the faith. Dr. Brooks reported, "Though she had never heard a word from the outside world about a Supreme Being, she responded 'I have been wishing for quite awhile that someone would teach me about Him. For I have been thinking about Him for a long time.'" Deep within her heart, God had instinctively put the desire for the eternal. John reminds us that *"He is the true light that gives light to every man."* John 1:9

My greatest comfort in the deaths of Tristan and Mandy was knowing that they knew the reality of John 3:16. *"For God so loved the word that He gave His one and only Son, that whoever believes in Him shall not perish but have eternal life."*

Only God Provides the Answers to Death

Moses was facing death when he said, "The eternal God is your refuge." Death is inevitable. It is no respecter of persons.

It is one of those fixed decrees of an unchanging God. It visits the rich and the poor, the sick and the healthy. No one is exempt! Visit the cemeteries of your city, and you will find all age groups represented there. As a pastor, I have stood by the graveside of a stillborn child, and I have been there with the aged saint. James said, "*Life is but a mist, a vapor, it appears for a moment and then vanishes away.*" I like the words of the song writer who said,

> *While I draw this fleeting breath,*
> *When my eyes shall close in death,*
> *When I rise to worlds unknown,*
> *And behold Thee on Thy throne,*
> *Rock of Ages, cleft for me,*
> *Let me hide myself in Thee.*[2]

Outside God's refuge, the world is an empty, lonely, cold place to live. This is especially true of those who do not know Christ when they come to the hour of death.

"*The sting of death is sin, and the power of sin is the law*" I Corinthians 15:56. In I Corinthians 15, Paul preaches the resurrection message. In this chapter, we discover:

1. Death is a passage.

2. Death is not the end.

3. Death is a new beginning.

We can face death with resurrection answers!

Only God Provides Strength for the Journey

"And underneath are the everlasting arms." Moses made this statement of affirmation based on personal experience. He had known the extremes of wealth and poverty. He had known joy and sorrow. Through every crisis in his life, Moses knew that God had provided answers. Now facing death, Moses knew that he would not have to cross death's chilling Jordan River alone. The strength and inner confidence that Moses verbalized in Deuteronomy 33:27 is reflected in the words of Tristan's mother just six days before he went to heaven.

> *I sit here in the darkened, quiet room, watching my son suffer silently. For six years he has battled valiantly against the cancer which is even now overtaking his brain. He doesn't cry or even ask why he should have to endure this, but spends his time endlessly telling us how much he loves everyone. As he approaches death, his main topic of conversation is love; his concern for others is now the controlling thought in his ever-dwindling "awake times." Jesus commanded us to "love one another as I have loved you — by this shall all men know ye are my disciples" John 13:34,35. Lord, thank you for teaching me discipleship through my child.*
>
> *Barbara Blann, January 10,1992*
> *Used with permission*

Life is tough, but God never fails to provide the assistance to see us through the most painful moments.

> *Ultimate Hope:*
> *That God is there,*
> *That God does care,*
> *That God can cope.*
>
> *June Bingham*

---

[1]Joseph M. Scriven (Words: ca 1855), Charles C. Converse (Music: ca 1855), "What A Friend We Have in Jesus" (Public Domain).
[2]Augustus M. Toplady (Words: 1776), Thomas Hastings (Music: 1830), "Rock of Ages" (Public Domain).

6

I've Gone to Look for Myself. If I Return
Before I Get Back, Ask Me to Wait.

Robb Robinson, a Tennessee state senator and funeral director, frequently shared humorous stories with me. One such story took place in Nashville.

A local minister, after officiating at a funeral, took the customary lead car position in the procession to the cemetery. It was during the Christmas season, and the pastor became preoccupied with thoughts of gifts he needed to purchase after the graveside services. When he approached the Spring Hill Cemetery, he looked left and saw the K– Mart store conveniently located across the street. Obviously lost in deep thought, he turned left into the K–Mart parking lot instead of the required right turn into the cemetery. As he drove through the parking lot looking for a parking space, he happened to look in his rear–view mirrow, and saw a string of cars following, all with their lights on!

Now that's really getting lost in deep thought!

I love fax machines. The title for this chapter is an edited version of one I received from an anonymous sender. Many times I receive faxes by mistake — but this one was written for me (and maybe the poor pastor who will never live down his trip through K– Mart!).

John Maxwell, noted author, lecturer and senior pastor of Skyline Wesleyan Church, has been my mentor for more than 20 years since I was privileged to serve as his first pastoral staff member at Faith Memorial Church in Lancaster, Ohio. John has guided me in matters of leadership, preaching, evangelism and church growth. Additionally, John, who is an excellent golfer, feels the need to mentor me in the great game of golf!

It was a rainy fall day, and I was busy working on a project when the intercom buzzer sounded. "Toler," the booming voice of Maxwell said, "Let's play 18!"

What a welcomed diversion! In a matter of minutes we loaded our golf clubs into John's 1972 Ford Pinto and hurried to the nearby Carrollwood golf course. Since it was raining steadily, the course was not crowded and we were able to tee off immediately.

For the first five holes, it appeared that the Maxwell Mentoring Course on golf was working. "What a great game — thanks for asking me to come along," I said to John.

As we approached the sixth tee box, I courageously asked John to loan me his three wood. He was proud of his new clubs but most willing to share them with his prized pupil. I stepped up to the tee box and took a practice swing. Feeling ready, I swung mightily at the little white ball.

To this day, I don't remember if I hit the ball, but what I do remember is the club slipping out of my hand and sailing 20 feet into the air! Embarrassing? You bet! And if that wasn't humbling enough, the three wood landed in a pine tree! Maxwell was in a state of unbelief.

"You just threw my new club in the tree! How on earth are we going to get it down?"

Mustering all the confidence I had, I said, "Give me your shoe." Obediently, John sat down on the cart and handed me his golf shoe. I threw his shoe up in the air in hopes of knocking the club out of the pine tree. To my dismay, his shoe got stuck in the same tree!

Undaunted, I said, "Give me your other shoe." Again, without arguing, John handed his other shoe to me. Taking better aim, I tossed his shoe at the club, and missed again! Unfortunately, the second shoe stayed in the tree, also.

As the drizzle became heavier, John stood up and said, "Toler, you big dummy! No, wait a minute — I'm the dummy! Stan, give me your shoe!"

In a spirit of fear and cooperation, I took off my shoe and handed it to him. And why not? He had a three–wood and two golf shoes in that pine tree! Taking careful aim, John threw my shoe at the club. Up it went, approximately 18 feet in the air, and missed everything. Feeling more confident, I picked up my shoe and tossed it at the club. It missed the club and fell downward, knocking one of John's shoes loose. Unfortunately, my shoe was now stuck in that tree! John instantly grabbed his shoe that had fallen to the ground. Now we had one golf club and a shoe each in that tree.

By this time, several other golfers had passed the sixth tee, observing this Laurel and Hardy comedy routine. Most did not speak or offer to help us. (Can you blame them?)

When all efforts failed in retrieving the golf club, my esteemed friend climbed the huge pine tree and retrieved the club and our shoes. Thunder could be heard in the background, and the rain was coming down harder. It seemed logical that we should quit for the day and go to the club house for hot chocolate.

Feeling somewhat embarrassed and helpless, we drove rapidly across the course to the clubhouse. As John opened the door, the room grew silent. Paranoia instantly gripped us. The other golfers had told on us — sure enough! As we stood in the doorway, laughter erupted like you've never heard. Quickly, I shut the door, and we left for home and dry clothes.

What a great example of life! We often get lost and cannot find our way. It may even appear that the whole world is laughing at our best effort. We feel so scared and unable to cope. Guidance from God is what we need. But how do we find such guidance?

Dr. James Dobson recently stated on his "Focus On the Family" radio broadcast, "There are few topics filled with as much confusion and contradiction as the subject of God's guidance." Many people view guidance from God in the same manner as a young man who tried to decide which young lady he should date. He began to pray to God for guidance in the matter. In his prayer, he said, "God, I'll flip a coin. You direct it. Heads it's Patty and tails it's Beatrice." He flipped his quarter and looked at it and saw that it was tails. He quickly prayed, "OK, God, how about two out of three?" Finding guidance from God is a greater process than flipping a coin or closing your eyes and pointing at random to a spot in your Bible.

When God shuts and bolts the door,
don't try to get in through the window.

Commit Your Plans to God

One of the most exciting aspects of our spiritual walk is to realize that God has a plan for each of His children. He has not left us to wander in the darkness of indecision. Solomon was very specific about the process of planning in Proverbs 16:1. *"...to men belong the plans of the heart, but from the Lord comes the reply of the tongue."* The message is clear. We may have our plans, but God wants to unfold His plans for our lives. *"In his heart a man plans his course, but the Lord determines his steps"* (verse 9).

"Commit to the Lord whatever you do, and your plans will succeed" Proverbs 16:3. What are we to commit? First, we are to commit our lives to Christ. Paul said of the Macedonians, "They gave themselves first to the Lord." Second, we are to commit our service to the Lord. God is interested in the work of our hands regardless of whether it takes place in Christian ministry, domestic situations or the marketplace. *"His intent was that now, through the church, the manifold wisdom of God should be made known to the rulers and authorities in the heavenly realms..."* (Ephesians 2:10). Before God shaped the world, He worked out the plan of servanthood.

I know the way God leads me, but well
do I know my Guide.
Martin Luther

Commit Your Abilities to God

The word *commitment* also involves faith. It is a frightening matter to talk about committing your abilities to God. We live in a time when few real commitments are made. Steve Farrar in *Point Man* said, "Commitment is cheap in marriage, business, politics, and even athletics. Commitment is cheap in professional sports when a running back will sign a six-year multi-million dollar contract and then stay out of training camp in his third year because the team won't renegotiate his contract. Why does he want to renegotiate? Because some other backs in the league recently signed new contracts worth more than his. He refuses to keep his commitment, until he gets his way. One player recently hinted that if his contract wasn't renegotiated, he wouldn't be able to give 100 percent on the field."[1]

You have been gifted by God to do His work. Doing service for God requires hard work and a definite commitment for life! There must never be a let-up in your spiritual walk with God.

Whenever you are seeking guidance from God, do not overlook your own gifts. God has given every believer at least one spiritual gift; therefore, when God calls on you to do something, you will be capable! He will not fail you at this point! You may be frightened by the opportunity, but God will energize your abilities.

We are often like the little girl who was afraid to go to bed in the dark by herself. After three or four trips to her parents' bedroom, her father sought to reassure her. "Look, honey," he said, "you are not really alone in your bedroom. God is watching over you. God is everywhere, and He is in your bedroom, too."

The little girl was not reassured by this. She started back to her room but stopped at the door and said in a loud whisper, "God, if you are in there, please don't say anything. It would scare me to death."

I remember the small frame church in Baileysville, West Virginia, where a revival meeting was held. The Tolers attended every service. I was just a 7-year-old boy, but one night I went to the altar to pray. Clearly and forcefully, I felt the call of God to preach. Was I frightened? Yes! It took me seven years to get the courage to tell another human being of God's call on my life. Thankfully by then, though, I knew that God had gifted me to preach the Gospel. Ultimately, at age 14, I committed my abilities to God, sought His guidance and surrendered to preach the Gospel.

God looks at you and sees a beautiful person waiting to be born! If you could see in a vision the man God meant you to be, never again could you be quiet. You'd rise up and try and succeed.

They tell us that ants are born with wings and use them, know the glory and flame and rapture of flight, then tear these wings off deliberately, choosing to live their lives out as crawling insects. Choosing that when God gave them the vast empire of the air! Don't make the same mistake by selling yourself short!

Dr. Norman Vincent Peale

"Brothers, think of what you were when you were called. Not many of you were wise by human standards; not many were influential; not many were of noble birth. But God chose the foolish things of the world to shame the wise; God chose the weak things of the world to shame the strong" I Corinthians 1:26, 27.

Commit Your Ministry to God

"Not everyone who says to me, 'Lord, Lord' will enter the kingdom of heaven, but only he who does the will of my Father who is in heaven" Matthew 7:21. It takes resolve to do the will of God.

Pastoring a church while a junior in high school caused me a great deal of pain and persecution. I was often called a "Jesus freak" and "Holy Boy." On one occasion, a student filled up the sink with water in the boys' restroom and said to me, "Come on, preacher boy, walk on water!" It didn't faze me, because I had resolved to follow Christ and preach His Word. Perhaps the words of a song written by my brother, Terry, describes my commitment:

> *I Will Live My Life for Christ*
> *(Chorus)*
>> *I will live my life for Christ*
>> *For me He paid such a price*
>> *My ambitions and plans are all in His hands*
>> *I will live my life for Christ*
>
> *(Verse 1)*
>> *You may spend your life seeking pleasure*
>> *Or filling your pockets with treasure*
>> *Living for yourself, Loving no one else*
>> *Living with no thought of forever*
>
> *(Verse 2)*
>> *I once lived my life that way*
>> *Then Jesus spoke sweet peace, one happy day*
>> *He made such a change, I praise His name*
>> *For He took all my sins away.*[2]

General William Booth, founder of the Salvation Army, was once asked, "What is the secret of your success?"

Booth responded, "From the day I got the poor of London on my heart and a vision of what Jesus Christ would do for them, I made up my mind that God should have all of William Booth there was; and if anything has been achieved, it is because God has had all the adoration of my heart, all the power of my will and all the influence of my life."

What a model for all who minister in Jesus' name! God wants 100 percent of you now!

Steps to Understanding God's Guidance

In *A Slow and Certain Light*, Elisabeth Elliott tells of two adventurers who stopped by to see her, all loaded with equipment for the rain forest east of the Andes. They sought no advice, just a few phrases to converse with the Indians.

She writes: "Sometimes we come to God as the two adventurers came to me — confident and, we think, well–informed and well–equipped. But has it occurred to us that with all our accumulation of stuff, something is missing?"

Elliott insists that we often ask God for too little. We know what we need: a yes or no answer, please, to a simple question. Or perhaps a road sign. Something quick and easy to point the way.

"What we really ought to have is the Guide Himself. Maps, road signs and a few useful phrases are good things, but infinitely better is Someone who has been there before and knows the way."

Step One: Be ready when God calls! My college president and hero in the faith, Dr. Melvin Maxwell, used to say, "We must be minutemen for the Lord." My personal formula for seeking God's guidance has always been pray, read God's word, listen for His call, go where He calls at a moment's notice!

> *"Ordinary people who make simple,*
> *spiritual commitments under the Lordship of Christ*
> *make an extraordinary impact on their world."*
>
> John Maxwell

Step Two: Be sure it's God calling! I've often prayed, "God, if this is you, I'm willing and ready, but if this feeling is a direct result of too much pepperoni pizza, I'll reject it!"

Some years ago, I was invited to speak in Oshkosh, Nebraska. I agreed to speak before I had the opportunity to speak with a travel agent. What a big mistake!

As the time of the speaking engagement approached, my secretary began to make my travel plans. Frustrated, she came into my office, complaining, "You can't get there from here!" And she was right! Traveling from Washington Court House, Ohio, to Oshkosh, Nebraska, was impossible. Immediately I picked up the phone and called the conference coordinator to tell him it would involve six plane changes, an overnight stay in Chicago, and lots of money!

Undaunted, he said, "Come on out! Everyone has difficulty getting to Oshkosh!"

The day finally arrived. As planned, I spent the night in Chicago, made a total of six stops and eventually landed in North Platte, Nebraska. A lovely pastoral couple met me at the airport, loaded me into their little Chevette Scooter, and then began the drive to Oshkosh. The two and one–half hours in a jam–packed Chevette Scooter even now causes me to pause and thank God that Chevrolet quit making those cars!

After the luggage surrounding me was removed, I unfolded my 5'8" frame and climbed out of the car. Greeted warmly by everyone, I walked toward the little white frame church building. As I entered the front door, I noticed a sign. It read: "There's no other place anywhere near this place like this place — this must be the place!" Naturally, I laughed heartily after all I had gone through to get to Oshkosh!

God really spoke to me through that sign on the church door. The message was crystal clear: God's place of service is the best place in the world! With so much dissatisfaction in our world, we must learn to be content with our place of ministry.

Having served in churches in several states over nearly 30 years of ministry, I can tell you that I have applied the words of the great Apostle Paul to each place of service. Paul said, *"I have learned to be content whatever the circumstances"* Philippians 4:11. He continues in verses 12 and 13, *"I know what it is to be in need, and I know what it is to have plenty. I have learned the secret of being content in any and every situation, whether well-fed or hungry, whether living in plenty or in want. I can do everything through him who gives me strength."*

So many believe that the grass is greener on the other side and often pursue that other side. I think, however, that Erma Bombeck, the great "folk theologian," had it right when she said, "The grass is always greener over the septic tank!" This is especially true when you are living outside the will of God.

My value, my self–esteem, and happiness are all found in God's place!

Step Three: Clarify the guidance. Is it yes? Is it no? Should I get help quick? Can I find scriptural backing or is this totally contrary to His Word? God will never tell you to do anything wrong!

Perhaps this story about a junior high Sunday school teacher will emphasize the importance of being clear about God's guidance.

The teacher of this junior high class was trying to illustrate the word *miracle*.

"Boys and girls," he said, "Suppose I stood on the roof of a 10–story building, lost my balance and fell off. Then all of a sudden, in midair, a whirlwind swept me up and brought me safely to the ground. Now what word would you use to describe this?"

After a long silence a boy raised his hand and asked, "Luck?"

"True, true," replied the minister. "It could be luck. But that's not the word I wanted. I'll repeat the story. There I am on top of the 10–story building again, and I fall. A whirlwind catches me in midair and places me safely on the ground. Think now, what word would describe the situation?"

"Accident," cried out one girl.

"No, no," answered the teacher. "Listen carefully for the third time. I'm on that same building, I fall and am swept to safety by a sudden whirlwind. What word could account for my safely reaching the ground?"

The boys and girls shouted in unison: "Practice!"

Step Four: Obey the message. If God tells you to do it, by all means do what He says, or you will be sorry.

One foggy night the captain of a large ship saw what appeared to be another ship's running lights approaching in the distance. The other ship was evidently on a collision course with his ship, so the captain quickly signaled to the approaching ship,

"Please change your course 10 degrees west." The reply returned back, blinking through the fog.

"You change your course 10 degrees east."

The captain became furious and shot a message back to the other ship, "I'm a sea captain with 35 years experience. You change your course 10 degrees west!" Without waiting, the signal flashed back, "I'm a seaman fourth class. You change your course 10 degrees east!"

Enraged and incensed, the captain knew that he was heading for a terrible head on crash. He blazed a last message to the fast approaching ship: "I'm a 50,000 ton freighter. You change your course 10 degrees west!"

The simple message winked back, "I'm a lighthouse. You change..."[3]

Recently, I have developed a newfound friendship with Dwight "Ike" Reighard, a Southern Baptist pastor from Georgia. While eating in one of Fayetteville's "meat and three" restaurants, Ike began to share about the loss of both his wife and baby due to a pregnancy complication.

Recovering from grief, he discovered, is like climbing a ladder one rung at a time. At first he asked, "Why?" Then he asked, "Why me?" Finally, after much prayer and help from a Christian counselor, he came to the conclusion that while he did not understand why they died, he needed to focus on the *what* instead of the *why*. He asked, "God, what message of guidance do you have for me?" Ike then began to acknowledge his needs and fill them with God's guidance.

Step Five: Give thanks to God for the call. *"His divine power has given us everything we need for life and godliness through our knowledge of Him who called us by His own glory and goodness"* II Peter 1:3.

Joyce Hollyday stated in an article for *Sojourners*, "A hazard of communities and people with a vocation to seek the kingdom of God and to work for justice is to forget to celebrate what we have, as well as what we haven't. We see what we have not accomplished, what is wrong and what we lack, but it is more awkward for us to give thanksgiving and praise. We may fear being accused of being naive. Often those who are materially poor have attitudes of praise which markedly affect their lives. Little children's prayers are almost exclusively prayers of thanksgiving. In the gospel, faith and praise are intimately linked."[4]

She is so right. Receiving guidance from God involves a simple child–like faith. Therefore, our response to God's call must always include thanksgiving and praise.

Too many believers fail to give thanks when God calls. It is important to give thanks, because we are told to do so in the word of God. Further, if we have experienced the in–filling of the Holy Spirit, we will consistently thank God for all things.

It is my firm belief that when we fail to give thanks to God for His call, we step out of His will for our lives. Paul warns Timothy in II Timothy 3:1, 2, *"But mark this: there will be terrible times in the last days. People will be lovers of themselves, lovers of money, boastful, proud, abusive, disobedient to their parents, ungrateful, unholy..."* With this in mind, we should never offer prayers to God without offering words of thanksgiving and praise.

Why should we give thanks? Because it is our entrance into God's throne room. Norman Vincent Peale coined the phrase *thanks–living*. I believe thanksliving was practiced by the early Christians and must become a daily ritual in the lives of 20th century believers.

Always thank God for His guidance, even when you don't particularly like it! God knows what's best for you.

> *"To know the will of God is our greatest knowledge.*
> *To do the will of God is our greatest achievement."*
> *George Truett*

[1]Steve Farrar, *Point Man*, (Portland: Multnomah, 1990), p. 56.

[2]Terry N. Toler (Words and Music: 1969), "I Will Live My Life for Christ."

[3]Dennis Rainey, *Building Your Mate's Self–Esteem* (San Bernardino: Here's Life, 1986), pp. 56, 57.

[4]Joyce Hollyday, "Gratitude", *Sojourners*, June 1987, pp. 32, 33.

7

Life's Adventure in Wonder Land

"...unless you change and become like little children you will never enter the kingdom of heaven."
Matthew 18:3

I'll never forget when our family moved from West Virginia to Ohio and all the changes that we experienced. Not only did we have "indoor plumbing" for the first time, but also instead of having a coal stove for cooking, we had a gas stove with an oven. That was quite a change for my mother. Excitedly, she went to the grocery store and purchased a canned ham. Mom read the instructions, preheated the oven to 425°, and placed the canned ham in the oven (can and all!). Mom smiled sweetly and said, "Off we go to church; our ham will be ready when we get back!"

After church we hurried home, looking forward to eating our cooked ham. But to our dismay, we discovered that our canned ham was just a bit "overcooked." It had exploded in the oven, blown off the oven door and sent most of the ham to the ceiling! Change is difficult, even for mothers!

The dictionary defines change as "putting something in place of something else." Change is the process of alteration and replacement.

Our world is changing at a frightening pace. A newspaper columnist described America 190 years ago. "Life expectancy was 38 years; the average work week was 72 hours; and the median annual wage was $300.00. On occasion, epidemics claimed the lives of entire families. Rivers carried cholera, typhoid, and yellow fever, and one of these diseases killed one out of five residents of Philadelphia in 1793.[1]

Change is never easy. Senior friends have told me that when trains were first introduced, many naysayers predicted that passengers would get nosebleeds because the trains were traveling at the speed of 15 miles per hour. Additionally, real concern was expressed that travelers might suffocate when going through tunnels.

Even the birth of the telephone was an exasperating experience for business leaders. Joshua Coppersmith was arrested in Boston for attempting to sell stock in a company that would design and build telephones. His arrest was based on the fact that "well–informed people know it is impossible to transmit the human voice over a wire."

Are you struggling with all the changes taking place in the world today? Is the whole process frightening to you? Well, get ready—more changes are ahead for you!

Not in the lifetime of most men has there been so much grave and deep apprehension...The domestic economic situation is in chaos. Our dollar is weak throughout the world. Prices are so high as to be utterly impossible. Of our troubles man can see no end.

Harpers Weekly, 1857

The 1990 U.S. Census revealed even more startling changes. For example, 100 years ago, 50 percent of the labor force was in agriculture and only 2 percent was in information, communication and publication. Today, the exact reverse is true! Not only has what people do changed, but so has how they do it. According to Harper's index, the average American will hold eight different jobs and live in more than 30 different houses during his/her lifetime.

Michael Kami, in his book, *Trigger Points*, used Coca–Cola as an illustration of rapid change. Just a few years ago Coca–Cola sold two kinds of drinks, Coca–Cola and Tab. Today, the same company markets New Coke, Coca–Cola Classic, Diet Coke, Caffeine–Free Coke, Caffeine–Free Diet Coke, Cherry Coke, Diet Cherry Coke and Tab, with or without calcium. It is also available in 42 different kinds of containers.

That's quite a change from Henry Ford's philosophy about his favorite product. "You can have a car any color you want as long as it's black!" Future generations will look back on this decade as a time of great change.

Probably the best example of change, though, is McDonald's. Hardly a two–week period passes without something new or something different going on at McDonald's: a new product, an incredible offer, a new game, a new gift. "We can invent," Ray Kroc once said, "faster than the others can copy."[2]

But it doesn't stop with Coca–Cola and McDonald's. Change touches on almost every aspect of life. While change is not always welcomed, it does not have to be a bad experience. Some change can be good.

In the January 1994 issue of *McCall's* magazine, Dr. Judith Sills listed eight amusing signs that indicate you might need to change:

1. The counter boy at Dunkin' Donuts greets you by name.

2. Dust balls fall out when you unroll your exercise mat.

3. On Monday you start wishing for Friday.

4. You often lose patience with your children and your co-workers.

5. It has been two years since you tried a new cologne.

6. You keep saying you'll sign up for stenciling lessons, but never do.

7. All you seem to do on Saturdays is run errands.

8. A sunset doesn't take your breath away.[3]

The book, *I'm OK, You're OK*, was required reading during my college days. Tom Harris, the famous psychiatrist who wrote this enormously successful book, said there are three reasons people change. First, people change when it is more painful to remain as they are. Perhaps you are in a job that is very painful to you. You cannot imagine being in that job for the rest of your life, so you make a change because it is more painful to stay where you are than to change.

A second time for change, according to Harris, is when we find ourselves at the point of despair. Perhaps we suddenly come to the realization that we are about to lose our marriage, our job, our health. At that point we may change. You have probably heard people say, "I had to reach rock bottom before I could take hold of my life."

Harris believes that there is a third motive for change. He calls it the "Eureka Stage." That is, some people change because they discover—much to their surprise—that there is something better that they have been missing. Of course, this is the message of the Gospel. There is a richer, fuller life that is available to all who will receive it.[4]

Genesis Chapter 32 records an incident in the life of Jacob that beautifully illustrates the positive aspects of change. Truth is, if we are honest, all of us would change something about ourselves.

"So Jacob was left alone, and a man wrestled with him until daybreak. When the man saw that he could not overpower him, he touched the socket of Jacob's hip so that his hip was wrenched as he wrestled with the man" Genesis 32:24–25. The Bible gives us a view from God's perspective. Someone has said, "He doesn't change us so that He can accept us. He accepts us so that He can change us!"

> *"In the end, it is important to remember that we cannot become what we need to be by remaining what we are."*[5]
> Max Dupree

As a young kid, I enjoyed big–time TV wrestling. Some of my favorite wrestlers were Dusty Roads, The Sheik and Cocoa Brazil. On Saturday afternoon, my brothers and I gathered around the black and white TV set and watched wrestling. During the TV commercials, we often stripped down to our boxer shorts and practiced our own wrestling skills. Being the older, stronger brother, I usually won the match. If my brother, Terry, ended up on the bottom of the pile, our little brother, Mark, jumped on top of me and the fight was on! We'd fight until someone yelled, "Uncle!"

I'll never forget one Saturday after the "fights," I was especially energized by the television match. During the commercial break, I picked Terry up and threw him across the room. There was silence. Terry was not breathing! "He's dead!" I thought. I fell to my knees and cried out to God for forgiveness. I began to weep and cry aloud, "Oh, Terry, forgive me. I'm going to jail, I didn't mean to kill my brother."

Suddenly, Terry rolled over, began laughing and pounded the floor with enthusiasm. "I tricked you! I fooled you!" he shouted. Well, the fight was on again in a matter of seconds.

"Uncle!" he yelled. It's a good thing, too—I think I had murder in my heart!

Jacob the swindler, cheater and manipulator was changed through a wrestling match with an angel. As God dealt with Jacob in a one–on–one match, Jacob caught a glimpse of what his life could become through change.

Changed Through A Crisis

What are you wrestling with this week? Shad Helmstetter, in his book *You Can Excel In Times of Change*, discusses the major changes we face in life. He focuses on matters of loss, separation, health, relationships and personal growth. Then he enumerates these steps for dealing with the matter of change:

1. Recognize and understand the change you are going through.

2. Accept or reject the change. That is, decide how you are going to let the change affect you.

3. Choose your attitude toward this change. We cannot always choose the changes, but we can always choose our attitude toward the change.

4. Choose your style of handling the change. Will you use acquiescence, active resistance, or positive acceleration?

5. Choose your action. Set out a strategy for dealing with the change.

6. Review, evaluate, and adjust as you go along.[6]

In a *Peanuts* comic strip, Lucy is walking along the road with Charlie Brown, who asks her, "Lucy, are you going to make any New Year's resolutions?" Lucy hollers back at him, knocking him off his feet: "What? What for? What's wrong with me now? I like myself the way I am! Why should I change? What in the world is the matter with you, Charlie Brown? I'm all right the way I am! I don't have to improve. How could I improve? How, I ask you? How?"[7]

> *"Everyone thinks of changing the world, but*
> *no one thinks of changing himself."*
> Leo Tolstoy

Changed Through Persistence

Then the man said, "Let me go, for it is daybreak." But Jacob replied, 'I will not let you go unless you bless me' Genesis 32:26. God often waits to resolve a problem to see if we really mean business. Have you ever looked up to God and said, "God, if you'll get me out of this mess, I promise I'll change!" Jacob was finished being a spiritual sprinter! He was ready to make a commitment to worship the true and living God. He was essentially saying, "I won't cry 'Uncle!' until you bless me!" In this day of instant grits, instant coffee, and microwave popcorn, we must remember that spiritual worship does not come without prayer, fasting and agonizing before God.

Harold Sherman wrote a book entitled, *How to Turn Failure Into Success*. In it, he gives a code of persistence. He says:

1. I will never give up so long as I know I am right.

2. I will believe that all things will work out for me if I hang on to the end.

3. I will be courageous and undismayed in the face of odds.

4. I will not permit anyone to intimidate or deter me from my goals.

5. I will fight to overcome all physical handicaps and setbacks.

6. I will try again and again and yet again to accomplish what I desire.

7. I will take new faith and resolution from the knowledge that all successful men and women have had to fight defeat and adversity.

8. I will never surrender to discouragement or despair no matter what seeming obstacles may confront me.

Jacob wrestled with the decision to commit to real-life priorities. I especially enjoy the story of the family who decided to leave the city and move to the country. They bought a ranch and made plans to raise cattle. They completed the relocation process and set about building their ranch, and about six months later, friends came to see them. They wanted to see the ranch and the cattle. The friend said to the owner of the ranch, "What do you call the ranch?" The owner of the ranch said, "I wanted to call it the 'Flying W.' My wife wanted to name it the 'Suzie Q.' But my oldest son wanted to call it the 'Bar J.' And my youngest son wanted to call it the 'Lazy Y Ranch.'"

So, he said, "What *did* you call it?"

"Well, we called it 'The Flying W, Suzie Q, Bar J, Lazy Y Ranch,'" he said.

"Ok, " the friend said, "but where's the cattle?"

The owner said, "Well, we don't have any. None of them survived the branding." If cattle cannot survive the branding of misplaced priorities, then neither can you. You're just going to be wounded, beaten up, bruised, battle-scarred, defeated and discouraged most of the time. When you get your priorities in order, you will cry out, "God, does my life please you?"

Jacob said, "I will not let you go..." He was ready to put God first in his life even if it would cost him everything. Jacob paused to worship God in a time of unparalleled crisis. He was willing to let God change him.

You can change, too! It doesn't matter whether you are poor, physically limited, filled with hatred, are manipulative — you don't have to stay bound and oppressed by Satan.

You are God's child. He will help you break the chains of sin and overcome the enemy! Satan will be the one who cries, "Uncle!"

"You are the way you are because that's the way
you want to be. If you really wanted to be different,
you would be in the process of changing right now."
Fred Smith

Changed Through Confession

"The man asked him, 'What is your name?' 'Jacob,' he answered"
Genesis 32:27. I've often wondered, Why this question? The
name Jacob means "heel catcher" or "deceiver." It is my personal
belief that he answered, "Jacob" in order to confess his sinfulness
as a person. If you were to confess your own character flaws,
what would they be? Tough question? You bet! There's a big-
time wrestling match going on for your soul! When you confess
your weaknesses to God, you are on your way to spiritual
victory!

Martin Luther, the great leader of the Reformation, was in his
study one day preparing to preach when he wrote, "Satan came
into my study.

While I was seated at my desk studying the word of God,
Satan walked into the room with a huge scroll under his arm. He
stopped me in the middle of my studies and said, 'Martin Luther,
listed on this scroll are all the sins that you've ever committed.
Read your sins, Martin Luther, read them!'

Satan held the scroll up by one end and forced me to read all
the sins that I had committed in my entire life. Finally after
about an hour of reading all the sinful things that I had done, it
seemed as though Hell was going to open up and I was going to
fall down into the horrible pit. In desperation, I reached out and
took hold of the scroll and unrolling it one more turn, I read,

"'But the blood of Jesus Christ, God's Son, cleanses us from all sin.'"

The Bible clearly teaches, "If we confess our sins, He is faithful to forgive our sins!"

Changed Through Worship

"Jacob said, 'Please tell me your name.' But he replied, 'Why do you ask my name?' Then he blessed him there. So Jacob called the place Peniel, saying, 'It is because I saw God face to face, and yet my life was spared'" Genesis 32:29, 30. Jacob faced God, confessed his weaknesses, and committed his life. A new name was given to Jacob; his name became Israel, which means two things: "He who struggles with God," and "Prince of God." The moment Jacob began to worship God, a new name was written down in heaven! *"Therefore, if anyone is in Christ, he is a new creation; the old has gone, the new has come!"* II Corinthians 5:17

Praise and worship is the key to the heart of God. Why not pause for a moment and focus on the following praise verses:

Psalm 8:2 *"From the lips of children and infants you have ordained praise because of your enemies, to silence the foe and the avenger."*

Psalm 34:1 *"I will extol the Lord at all times; his praise will always be on my lips."*

Psalm 48:1 *"Great is the Lord, and most worthy of praise, in the city of our God, his holy mountain."*

Psalm 145:21 *"My mouth will speak in praise of the Lord. Let every creature praise his holy name for ever and ever."*

Psalm 150:1, 2 *"Praise the Lord. Praise God in his sanctuary; praise him in his mighty heavens. Praise him for his acts of power; praise him for his surpassing greatness."*

James 5:13 *"Is any one of you in trouble? He should pray. Is anyone happy? Let him sing songs of praise."*

Not long ago, my wife and I had lunch with Peggy Benson, wife of the late Bob Benson, who was one of my favorite writers. As we conversed, I told Peggy how much I enjoyed her new book, *Listening For A God Who Whispers*. As we continued to talk, the conversation moved to the matters of loneliness and grief. Peggy began to share how she had built altars throughout her house. She revealed the various ways in which she practiced the presence of God through worship. Peggy told me that she was overcoming her grief and feelings of loneliness through the worship of God and a simple faith in the promises of God. She cited Ephesians 3:17, *"...so that Christ may dwell in your hearts through faith. And I pray that you, being rooted and established in love...,"* as her scripture of choice for her home. Peggy concluded our luncheon with these poignant words: "Every day I celebrate the presence of Christ in my home, and I am not alone!"

Changed Through Trust

"The sun rose above him as he passed Peniel, and he was limping because of his hip" Genesis 32:31. Have you ever wondered why Jacob walked with a limp the rest of his life? Many scholars believe that his physical disability was a reminder of his need to trust God on a daily basis. Are you like Jacob? Do you need to change? You cannot do it alone. You must have God's help!

Don Bennett, a Seattle businessman, decided to climb Washington's Mount Ranier. It's a stiff climb to the peak of the

14,410–foot summit, but so many individuals have made the climb that it no longer merits getting their names in the newspaper. For Don Bennett, however, the climb was a remarkable achievement, and papers nationwide carried the news. He was the first amputee ever to reach Mount Ranier's summit.

In the book, *The Leadership Challenge*, Barry Posner tells the story of how Bennett made the climb on one leg and two crutches. Asked by reporters to share the most important lesson he learned from his celebrated climb, Bennett spoke of the team of individuals who helped him attain his dream. "You can't do it alone," he said.

"When you're through changing, you're through."
Bruce Barton

Three years ago, my wife and I sat in her hospital room waiting for Dr. Michael Santi, her physician, to visit with us. She had been diagnosed with colon cancer and was scheduled for surgery the next day.

He entered Linda's room with his usual smile, sat down on the edge of her bed and proceeded to explain what would take place in the operating room the following morning. Frankly, we were scared to death! But when he finished explaining the surgery, recovery time, etc., he calmly took Linda by the hands and held them heavenward.

"Linda," he said, "tomorrow our hands will be in His hands." Then he prayed the most magnificent prayer for my wife. "God, I cannot do this alone. I need your help," he said.

This was our first indication that Dr. Santi was a believer. What a God! In the midst of our frightening experience, God gave us a Christian doctor!

As I write this, I am seated in a waiting room of that same hospital. Linda has just had her annual check–up. It has been exactly three years since she had colon cancer surgery. Dr. Santi smiles as he enters the room.

"I have good news for you. Your wife is doing great—no sign of cancer or polyps anywhere!"

Yes, through the hands of a skilled surgeon, the prayers of God's people and the encouragement of loved ones, my wife has been healed.

In retrospect, I can testify that we were "changed" through this event. While cancer is certainly a cruel disease, God is greater than any health problem we may encounter. You can trust Him with your troubles!

> *He's the Master of the mighty*
> *He's the Captain of the conquerors*
> *He's the Head of the heroes*
> *He's the Leader of the legislators*
> *He's the Overseer of the overcomers*
> *He's the Governor of Governors*
> *He's the Prince of princes*
> *He's the King of kings*
> *He's the Lord of lords!*
> *YOU CAN TRUST HIM!*
> S.M. Lockridge

Throughout Linda's bout with cancer, we were encouraged to trust God through five very simple ways:

1. The prayers of God's people.

2. The presence of our family members.

3.   A Christian doctor.

4.   The ministry of several pastor friends, but especially Ken Southerland, who drove 700 miles to minister to us.

5.   Cards and letters, especially the one reprinted below.   It was sent to me by a cancer patient, Irene Williams, who is now in heaven where she has perfect health!

WHAT CANCER CAN'T DO

Cancer is so limited...

> *It cannot cripple love, it cannot shatter hope,*
> *It cannot corrode faith, it cannot eat away peace,*
> *It cannot destroy confidence,*
> *It cannot kill friendship,*
> *It cannot shut out memories*
> *It cannot silence courage,*
> *It cannot invade the soul,*
> *It cannot reduce eternal life,*
> *It cannot quench the spirit,*
> *It cannot lessen the power of the resurrection.*

Though the physical body may be destroyed by disease, the spirit can remain triumphant. If disease has invaded your body, refuse to let it touch your spirit. Your body can be severly afflicted, and you may have a struggle. But if you keep trusting God's love, your spirit will remain strong.

Why must I bear this pain? I cannot tell; I only know my Lord does all things well. And so trust in God, my all in all, for He will bring me through, what'er befall.

Our greatest enemy is not disease, but despair.

Source Unknown

As a result of the "cancer crisis" in our home, I have reached the conclusion that all good things come from God's hand. Our home, children, food, flowers, music, sunsets, rain, snow, and most of all LIFE, reflect his unconditional love.

Please pray this simple prayer with me:

"Lord, as I begin this new day, I am resolved to break free of Satan's chains and *change* I am your expectant child. Please let your Holy Spirit work in my life to change me for the better. In Jesus' name. Amen!"

---

[1] Ernest A. Fitzgerald, *God Writes With Crooked Lines*, (New York: Atheneum, 1981).

[2] Daniel S. Kennedy, *The Ultimate Marketing Plan*, (Massachusetts: Bob Adams, Inc.).

[3] Judith Sills, Ph.D., "10 Ways to Get the Most From Your Relationships", (*McCalls*, January, 1994), p. 68.

[4] Tom Harris, *I'm OK, You're OK*, (New Jersey: Revell Publishers, 1973), p. 91.

[5] Max DuPree, *Leadership Is An Art*, (New York: Doubleday, 1989), p. 87.

[6] Shad Helmstetter, *You Can Excel in Times of Change*, (New York: Pocket Books, 1991), pp. 145-179.

[7] Rheta Grimsley Johnson, *Good Grief, the Story of Charles M. Schultz,* (New York: Pharos Books, 1989).

8

Never Check Your Oil While Parked on a Hill

It was a beautiful, sunny day. Not a cloud in the sky! The pilot, Tom Hawk, a World Relief Missions pilot, was busy showing David Vaughn and me the countryside. Flying from Ohio to Virginia can be an exhilarating experience! The mountains were breathtaking as we flew over my beloved West Virginia, and as we approached the Virginia border, it appeared that I would be right on schedule for my speaking engagement in Richmond.

In the distance, we could see heavy clouds, and rain began to descend on our Cherokee Piper. Nervously, our pilot called the Richmond tower. That's when we discovered that he wasn't instrument–rated.

For the next hour, Tom spoke with the air controller, who guided us skillfully down through the clouds and to the ground. The moments in the sky were so tense that no one mentioned the potential danger we were facing. But, as we got out of the plane, my friend, David, as pale as a ghost, knelt down and kissed the pavement! "Now I know why the Pope kisses the ground every time he gets out of a plane!" he said. He had echoed my sentiments exactly. I had been scared to death! What tremendous relief to be safe on the ground again!

> *Don't despair. Even the sun has a*
> *sinking spell every night,*
> *but it rises again in the morning!*

Franklin Roosevelt, while assistant secretary to the Navy, was stricken with polio. Through exercise and therapy, he was able to regain the use of his hands and was able to shuffle his feet and take a few steps with the use of a brace. Friends encouraged him to back off and take life easy. Although he could have done that because he was a very wealthy man, he was determined to become a public servant. Soon he became governor of New York. Eleven years later, he became the 32nd president of the United States.

Roosevelt was also a man who admittedly had a fear of fire. He was especially afraid that he would be in his office in his wheelchair and would not be able to get out of the building if it caught fire. On the day of his inauguration as president, he shuffled to the podium and said, "We have nothing to fear but fear itself." He made that statement in light of the fact that one of every four men in America was unemployed, and America was in the midst of a great depression.

Recently I had the privilege of eating dinner with Rick Stanley, the step–brother of Elvis Presley, and Dr. Nelson Price, pastor of the great First Baptist Church of Roswell, Georgia, for the past 30 years. The conversation moved from stories by Rick Stanley about his brother, Elvis, to Civil War stories told by Dr. Price.

As Dr. Price recounted a Stone Mountain Civil War showdown, he began to talk about the anxieties that plagued the Confederate soldiers. I was captivated by a statement that he made about fear. He said, "Fear robs the mind of reason and the ability to act!"

Without doubt, we live in a world of fear. According to psychiatrist, James Reich, in *The Journal of Nervous and Mental Disease*, 3 percent of the population of the United States experience panic, 6 percent agoraphobia, 3 percent generalized anxiety, more than 2 percent simple phobias (fear of a specified situation, object, creature, activity, or experience), and nearly 2 percent social phobias (dread of situations in which they may be observed by others in such acts as eating, speaking, writing, vomiting, or urinating). Research by the National Institute of Mental Health shows that phobias and related anxiety disorders are the *most common psychological problems* in America. More than 13 million people are affected.[1]

Donald Medeiros stated in his book, *Children Under Stress*, that "more than six out of 10 children, in our land, between the ages of 7 and 11 report that they are afraid someone will break into their house and hurt them." After interviewing 2,200 children, Medeiros concluded in his book that "25 percent of the children said that they were afraid they might be hurt when they left their house. And in all types of neighborhoods more than 50 percent of the children said they think their neighborhood is not a very good place to grow up."[2]

In a recent survey, *Psychology Today* polled its readers to find out what they were afraid of. More than 1,000 responded. Elizabeth Stark wrote, "Respondents chose death of a loved one overwhelmingly as their greatest fear. This was followed by serious illness. Financial worries and nuclear war tied for third."[3]

Denis Waitley, in his book *Seeds of Greatness*, tells of a study done at the University of Michigan on fear in relationship to reality. The study indicated that 60 percent of our fears are totally unwarranted; that is, the things we fear never come to pass. 20 percent of our fears have already become past activities. That is, they are completely out of our control. 10 percent of our fears are so petty they don't make any difference at all. Of the remaining 10 percent, only 4 to 5 percent are real and justifiable fears.[4]

Whether real or imagined, fears plague everyone! I enjoy stories about Vince Lombardi, the famous coach of the Green Bay Packers. Forrest Gregg, one of his toughest linemen, once stated, "Even the toughest of linemen was no match against Lombardi. When he said, 'Sit down!' we didn't even bother to look for a chair!"

Fear Is A Reality

"During the fourth watch of the night, Jesus went out to them, walking on the lake. When the disciples saw him walking on the lake, they were terrified. 'It's a ghost,' they said, and cried out in fear" Matthew 14:25, 26. Children in Bloomington, Illinois, were asked by their teacher, "If you could talk to President Lincoln, what would be the one question you would ask?" One child raised his hand and said, "I would ask him, 'Mr. Lincoln, were you afraid when you started first grade?'"

I can identify with that young man! In retrospect, I remember being afraid of rides at the circus. Once I was riding the Octopus, a fast-moving ride that went up and down so rapidly it took your breath away. "Let me off this ride," I screamed. "I'm sick!" The man attending to the ride found this humorous and despite my mother's plea to stop the ride, cranked it up another notch. Guess what? I threw up, people scurried for safety, and I stopped the ride!

Jim Wilcox told me the story of his twin brother, John, who also is terrified of roller coasters. Despite this overwhelming fear, however, Jim convinced John to join him on one during a recent visit to the Boardwalk in Santa Cruz, California. As the two–man car they rode reached the top of the first peak, Jim noticed that John was gripping the bar so tightly his knuckles were nearly glowing white. When Jim turned to tease John about his phobic behavior, he saw John's lips moving, but it wasn't until they started down that first drop at 50 miles per hour that his whisper reached a crescendo: "I hate you! I hate you! I hate you!!"—a refrain he was to continue throughout his entire ordeal.

Still another time of great fear in my life came when my father was killed in a construction accident. I feared everything — teachers, changing classes, sleeping alone at night, and the neighborhood bully! As I moved into my teen years, another fear plagued me: working on my 1959 Rambler. I have never been mechanical (I can barely make toast), but I had received instructions from my stepfather to check my oil regularly. So, I did. The first time I checked the oil in my Rambler, it was parked on the side of a hill and the dipstick showed EMPTY! Boy, was I scared! I hurried to the nearest filling station to pour in a quart of 10–W–40 only to discover through a helpful attendant that my dipstick now registered full. I thought it was a miracle! I later found out that you should never check your oil while parked on a hill.

> *Don't be afraid of the day you have never seen.*
> English Proverb

Fear goes back to Adam when he said, *"I heard you in the garden and I was afraid"* Genesis 3:10. Yes, many of our fears are genuine. Harold Kushner, in his book *When All You've Ever Wanted Isn't Enough*, clarifies the difference between fear and awe.

> Fear is a negative emotion. It is constricting. It makes us either want to run away from whatever we are afraid of, or destroy it. It makes us feel angry and resentful, angry at the person or thing that frightens us and angry at our own weakness which leaves us vulnerable. To obey God out of fear is to serve Him sullenly and with only part of ourselves.

> But awe is a positive feeling, an expansive feeling. Where fear makes us want to run away, awe makes us want to draw closer even as we hesitate to get too close. Instead of resenting our own smallness or weakness, we stand open–mouthed in appreciation of something greater than ourselves. To stand at the edge of a steep cliff and look down is to experience fear. We want to get out of that situation as quickly and safely as we can. To stand securely on a mountaintop and look around us is to feel awe. We could linger there forever.[5]

Peter, still terrified, cried out, *"Lord, if it's you, tell me to come to you on the water. 'Come,' he said. Then Peter got down out of the boat, walked on the water and came toward Jesus. But when he saw the wind, he was afraid and, beginning to sink, cried out, 'Lord, save me!'"* Matthew 14:28-30. Peter looked to Christ and began walking once again on the water. The key to victory over your fears is your focus on God. Keep your eyes on Him, and you will stay on top of your fears.

> *The Bible repeats the command,*
> *"Fear not!" hundreds of times.*

Fear Is Related to Doubt

"Immediately, Jesus reached out his hand and caught him. 'You of little faith,' He said, 'Why did you doubt?'" Matthew 14:31.

> *Both faith and fear may sail into your harbor,*
> *but allow only faith to drop anchor.*

When Peter lost his focus, he began to doubt. My guess is that Peter didn't know how to swim! He began to sink, and, scared to death, he cried out, "Lord save me!"

The word *fear* comes from the Old English *faer*, meaning sudden danger. It refers to fright where fright is justified. It refers to danger that is concrete, real and knowable. In such cases, fear is appropriate and sometimes useful if one is to escape harm.

In an interview Steve Allen once had with a doctor, Allen's guest said to him, "The only two really instinctive fears in men are the fear of loud noises and the fear of falling. What are you afraid of, Mr. Allen?"

Without skipping a beat, Steve Allen responded, "I have a great fear of making a loud noise while falling."

> *We always hope*
> *And in all things it is better*
> *To hope than to despair*
> *When we return to real*

Trust in
God there will
No longer be room in our
Soul for fear.

Goethe

Deliverance From Fear

Even legitimate fears can be given over to God! What is your greatest fear? Psalms 34:4 says, *"I sought the Lord, and He answered me, and delivered me from all my fears."* Don't you think that Peter, at the very moment Jesus reached out to him, thought of this psalm? Perhaps he began to hum Psalm 34 and thought, "Why did I doubt him in the first place?"

"All our fret and worry is caused by
calculating without God."

Oswald Chambers

We are reminded in II Timothy 1:7, *"For God did not give us a spirit of fear."* It is not God's plan to make us fearful. Every opportunity to be fearful is an opportunity to trust God!

Let me give you some steps to deliverance from fear.

1. Choose faith instead of doubt. Several years ago in Lancaster, Ohio, I heard Dr. E. Stanley Jones preach. He was a missionary statesman and a man of great faith, and his words of wisdom about overcoming worry and fear were so inspiring that I wrote them in the front of my New Testament:

I see that I am inwardly fashioned for faith and not for fear. Fear is not my native land; faith is. I am so made that worry and anxiety are sand in the machinery of life: faith is oil. I live better by faith and confidence than by fear and doubt and anxiety. In anxiety and worry, my being is gasping for breath — these are not my native air. But in faith and confidence, I breathe freely — these are my native air.

Perhaps you will recall the story of 18-year-old John Thompson from Hurdsfield, North Dakota. John had been working alone on the family farm. While operating a combine, his arms got caught, causing both to be amputated at the shoulder.

John freed himself from the machine and went to the farmhouse. Remaining calm, he managed to take the telephone off the hook with his teeth and, holding a pencil in his mouth, dialed 911. He then went and sat in the bathtub and waited for the emergency medical technicians to arrive. Why the bathtub? He didn't want to get blood on his mother's carpet!

When the ambulance arrived and the technicians saw John, they were horrified! John remained cool and collected. In fact, he instructed the technicians where to find his arms and even reminded them to pack them in ice from the family freezer.

Surgeons in Minneapolis, Minnesota, were able to re–attach John's arms, and as of this writing, he is doing extremely well.

What a courageous man! John could have laid down and died alone. But he chose not to. Instead he demonstrated his faith in God by willing himself to live and making the right decisions in the most difficult circumstances. His choice to live was rewarded greatly by God. What a bright future the youngster has!

> *"He can give only according to His might;*
> *therefore, He always gives more*
> *than we ask for."*

Martin Luther

2. Turn to God's Word for strength. The following verses have strengthened me in moments when I have been tempted to be fearful:

Psalm 34:7 *"The angel of the Lord encamps around those who fear him, and he delivers them."*

Genesis 26:24 *"Do not be afraid, for I am with you; I will bless you and will increase the number of your descendants for the sake of my servant Abraham."*

Psalm 23:4 *"Even though I walk through the valley of the shadow of death, I will fear no evil for you are with me; your rod and your staff they comfort me."*

Psalm 91:5 *"You will not fear the terror of night, nor the arrow that flies by day."*

I John 4:18 *"There is no fear in love. But perfect love drives out fear, because fear has to do with punishment. The one who fears is not made perfect in love."*

D.L. Moody used to say, "You can travel to heaven first class or second class. Second class is, *"What time I am afraid, I will trust"* Psalm 56:3. First class is, *"In God have I put my trust, I will not be afraid"* Psalm 56:11.

3. Find peace in the prayers of others. My friend, Doug Carter, was aboard USAir Flight 486 from Charlotte, North Carolina, to Columbus, Ohio, when at 31,000 feet over West Virginia, one of the engines exploded and blew a hole in the side of the plane. Doug described the gaping hole as about "three feet wide and six feet high." Oxygen masks began to drop, some passengers screamed while others prayed aloud as the plane went into a steep dive.

Doug told me that he felt sure that the plane would crash into the mountains, but more importantly, he said, "I had peace that I was ready to die." Incredibly, the severely damaged plane landed safely at the Charleston, West Virginia, airport. Airline spokespersons acknowledged that it had been a miracle.

Not long after this, Doug discovered from four separate individuals that they had been burdened to pray for him at the very hour his plane was enroute to Columbus, Ohio. God is never late when His children call out!

> Courage is fear that
> has said its prayers.

4. Ask God to deliver you from your fears. One thing I admire about Peter, even though he carried a reputation as a coward, was his ability to come back to Christ, always willing to admit his fears. Peter, gripped by fear, had cried out, "Lord, save me!"

> *"God has decreed to act in response to prayer.*
> *'Ask,' He commands us.*
> *And Satan trembles for fear we will."*
> *Ruth Bell Graham*

I grew up watching Ohio State football. I loved to go to the big horseshoe–shaped stadium and watch the Buckeyes play football. Woody Hayes, the dynamic, excitable and often controversial football coach, one day spoke at my Northland High School assembly. Coach Hayes concluded his speech by describing his first day as head coach of the Big Ten powerhouse.

"The first time I stood in the middle of the Ohio stadium with its 86,000 seats staring down at me, I was shook up. I stood there holding my son's hand and I thought of the fans and how angry they can get if you lose. Then I thought of all the people who were depending on me to develop a winning team. For a moment I felt fearful. My young son must have sensed my fear for he gripped my hand and said, 'Dad, look at the field, it's the same as all the others.'" Amazing, isn't it? A child calmed his father's fears.

If it's any encouragement to you, Jesus had fears, too. Please note what he had to say about His fears in Matthew 26:36-43:

> *"Then Jesus went with his disciples to a place called Gethsemane, and he said to them,. . .'Sit here while I go over there and pray'. . .He took Peter and the two sons of Zebedee along with him, and he began to be sorrowful and troubled. . .Then he said to them. . . 'My soul is overwhelmed with sorrow to the point of death. Stay here and keep watch with me. . .'*
>
> *Going a little farther, he fell with his face to the ground and prayed. . .'My Father, if it is possible, may this cup be taken from me. Yet not as I will, but as you will. . .'*
>
> *Then he returned to his disciples and found them sleeping. . .'Could you men not keep watch with me for one hour?. . .he asked Peter. . .Watch and pray so that you will not fall into temptation. . .The spirit is willing, but the body is weak. . .'*
>
> *He went away for a second time and prayed. . .'My Father, if it is not possible for this cup to be taken away unless I drink it, may your will be done. . .'*
>
> *When he came back, he again found them sleeping, because their eyes were heavy."*

God the Father heard his plea for help. The days ahead would not be easy for our Lord, but He knew He had the encouragement of the Father.

God already knows your fears. Ask Him to extend a calming hand to you right now. He will deliver you from your fears!

TRY GOD

When troubles are deep and your world is dark, don't give up hope,
"TRY GOD"...
When life turns sour and you've lost your way,
don't give up hope, "TRY GOD"...
When fears stack up and you're sure no one cares,
don't give up hope, "TRY GOD"...
When temptation comes knocking and
you struggle with it so,
don't give up hope, "TRY GOD"...

Source Unknown

---

[1]Robert Handly and Pauline Neff, *Beyond Fear*, (New York: Rawson Associates, 1987), p. 9.

[2]Donald C. Medeiros, et. al., *Children Under Stress*, (Englewood Cliffs, N.J.: Prentice–Hall Inc., 1983), pg. 89.

[3]John Haggai, *Winning*, (New York: Inspirational Press, 1991).

[4]Denis Waitley, *Seeds of Greatness*, (Old Tappan: Fleming H. Revell, Co., 1983), p. 76.

[5]Harold Kushner, *When All You've Ever Wanted Isn't Enough*, (New York: Penguin Books, 1986), pp. 130, 131.

9

When Nothing's Happening, Something's Happening

University of Illinois football coach, Bob Zuppke, was famous for his motivational half–time speeches. He really knew how to fire up his team!

One Saturday afternoon, Zuppke's team was losing and lethargic. Coach Zuppke gave a "win one for the Gipper" kind of speech. And the troops responded excitedly. Dramatically, the coach pointed to the door at the end of the locker room and said, "Now go out there and win this game!"

Emotionally charged, the players jumped up and ran to the door. The first player blasted through the door as several others followed. But it was the wrong door. One by one, they all fell into the swimming pool!

Life is a lot like that! We find a door, charge through it, only to discover it's the wrong door.

The phrase, "When nothing's happening, something's happening!" took on new meaning almost daily in my home mission church. I have often confided with friends that I enjoyed this faith–building experience more than any other phase of my ministry. It constantly required complete and utter dependence on God in the matter of church finances. We were always *broke!*

On one occasion, I took a step of faith and purchased on credit 22 used church pews at a cost of $2,000. This was a wonderful price considering new pews would have cost us approximately $8,000. I only had one problem — how on earth were we going to pay for the pews? After all, our church offerings only averaged $120 per week.

Thankfully, God was at work behind the scenes. Two years prior to this faith venture, I had written the Oldham Little Church Foundation requesting financial help with the construction of our church sanctuary. They responded quickly to my letter and turned us down. I accepted this disappointment and forgot about the whole situation.

I spent a very restless night walking the halls, crying, praying, and wondering why I had just spent $2,000 for those pews!

The very next morning, I stopped for my usual cup of coffee at Shoney's and then drove to the post office. There was only one envelope in the mail box, and it had a window. (Usually, this meant it was a bill!) I got into the car, tossed the letter aside and drove to my office. (I hate to open bills!) Later in the morning, I decided to open the letter. I was immediately stunned!

It was a letter from the Oldham Little Church Foundation, and it read:

"Dear Pastor Toler,

Greetings! I am writing to inform you of the decision of Oldham Little Church Foundation board to assist you in your building program. While the enclosed check is small, we trust that it will help you purchase some pulpit furniture.

Enclosed is a check for $2,000."

As I have reflected on this incident, I am reminded that God's timing is always perfect. He knows what we need and when we are in need. Personally, I have on occasion wished that He would work with my time schedule. But this I know: God is never late; God never fails!

The story is told of an Italian peasant man who encountered a monk from the monastery located on a mountain near his home village.

"Father," he said to the monk, "I've always wanted to ask something. What do you men of God do up on that huge hill?" The man continued, "Are you closer to God up on that mountain? Tell me about the life of holiness you live up there."

The wise monk was silent for a moment, stroked his beard and then said, "What do we men of God do up there on the holy mountain? I'll tell you what we do. We fall down, we get up. We fall down, we get up. We fall down, we get up. Quite humbling, don't you think, for holy men?"

Falling down is quite a humbling experience, yet it is very much a part of all of our lives. It certainly is essential to our spiritual development.

Learning to get along with others has its ups and downs. Mother Teresa, speaking at the National Prayer Breakfast in Washington, D.C., in 1993, said, "It is not enough for us to say, 'I love God,' but I also have to love my neighbor. St. John says that you are a liar if you say you love God, and you don't love your neighbor. How can you love God whom you do not see, if you do not love your neighbor whom you see, whom you touch, with whom you live? And so it is very important for us to realize that love, to be true, has to hurt. I must be willing to give whatever it takes not to harm other people and, in fact, to do good to them. This requires that I be willing to give until it hurts. Otherwise, there is no true love in me, and I bring injustice, not peace, to those around me."

Recently, I read an article that discussed the matter of theological forgiveness versus psychological forgiveness. The writer suggested that theological forgiveness was the ideal, because it speaks to us about the way God loves us, forgives us and forgets our sins. Psychological forgiveness, on the other hand, focuses on the need to forgive but also acknowledges the difficulty of forgetting.

I love to tell the story of little Johnnie, who was sitting on his front porch enjoying his candy bar when a so-called friend came by and took it from him. The friend ran down the street, eating the candy bar without shame. Johnnie chased him down, tackled him and sat down on his chest. Looking into his friend's chocolate-covered face, he said, "I could forgive you for stealing and eating my candy bar, but it would be easier to forget it if you would wipe the chocolate off your face!"

We all so desperately want forgiveness; we all so desperately need forgiveness. Both can be achieved through a clear understanding of the following verse.

"Be kind and compassionate to one another, forgiving each other, just as in Christ God forgave you" Ephesians 4:32.

> *"You cannot shake hands with a clenched fist."*
> Golda Meir

What Is Forgiveness?

Forgiveness means to conceal or send away. Romans 4:7, 8 says, *"Blessed are they whose transgressions are forgiven, whose sins are covered. Blessed is the man whose sin the Lord will never count against him."*

Richard Hoefler's book, *Will Daylight Come?* includes an insightful illustration of how sin enslaves and forgiveness frees.

A little boy visiting his grandparents was given his first slingshot. Johnny practiced in the woods, but he could never hit his target. As he came back to Grandma's back yard, he spied her pet duck. On an impulse, he took aim and let fly. The stone hit, and the duck fell dead. Johnny panicked. Desperately he hid the dead duck in the woodpile, only to look up and see his sister watching. Sally had seen it all, but she said nothing.

After lunch that day, Grandma said, "Sally, let's wash the dishes."

But Sally smiled, "Johnny told me he wanted to help in the kitchen today. Didn't you, Johnny?" And she whispered to him, "Remember the duck!" Johnny did the dishes.

Later Grandpa asked if the children wanted to go fishing. Grandma said, "I'm sorry, but I need Sally to help me make supper."

Sally grinned and said, "That's all taken care of. Johnny wants to do it." Again she whispered, "Remember the duck." Johnny peeled potatoes while Sally went fishing.

After several days of doing both his chores and Sally's, Johnny could stand it no longer. He confessed to his grandma that he'd killed the duck. "I know, Johnny," she said, giving him a hug. "I was standing at the window and saw the whole thing. Because I love you, I forgave you. I wondered how long you would let Sally make a slave of you."

> *"Jesus Christ knows the things you've done wrong,*
> *but He did not come to rub them in.*
> *He came to rub them out."[1]*
> Rick Warren

"Blessed is he whose transgressions are forgiven, whose sins are covered" Psalm 32:1.

Forgiveness Models the Life and Example of Christ

"*And when you stand praying, if you hold anything against anyone, forgive him, so that your Father in heaven may forgive you your sins*" Mark 11:25. Some years ago, while speaking at Houghton College, I had the privilege of meeting Dr. S.I. McMillen, author of *None of These Diseases*. Talking with Dr. McMillen was a stimulating experience. I shared with him that I had often quoted from his book and that perhaps his most challenging words to me centered on the matter of forgiveness, for he had once said, "The moment I start hating a man, I become his slave. He controls my thoughts. I cannot escape his grip on my mind. Hatred is a boomerang. It will return and find us instead of the intended target."

> *"Unforgiveness does a great deal more damage*
> *to the vessel in which it is stored than the object*
> *on which it is poured."*
>
> S.I. McMillen

Neil Anderson once said, We must forgive in the same way we have been forgiven. In His mercy, God has given us what we need, not what we deserve.

Forgiveness is hard for us because it goes against our sense of fairness. To forgive is a conscious decision of the will. Since God commands us to do it, we know that it is possible. We need to realize that forgiveness is not just for the sake of the offender, but also for ourselves — so that we can be free.

The high cost of forgiveness lies in the fact that it involves being willing to live with the consequences of someone else's sin. Genuine forgiveness is always substitutional, just as Jesus took upon Himself the penalty for our sin. That, in fact, is our motive for forgiving: He forgave us.[2]

Forgiveness is a command of Christ; therefore, every believer should endeavor to practice forgiveness. Perhaps Dr. Francis Schaffer said it best: "If I am not willing to practice forgiveness, then the world has a right to question whether Christianity is true."

I never knew a night so black
Light failed to follow on its track.
I never knew a storm so gray
It failed to have its clearing day.
I never knew such a black despair
That there was not a rift somewhere.
I never knew an hour so drear
Love could not fill it of cheer!

John Kendrick Bangs

"Forgiveness is not an occasional act;
it is a permanent attitude."

Martin Luther King, Jr.

Stages of Forgiveness

Lewis Smedes, preaching at Suncoast Community Church, stated that there are four stages to forgiveness:

Hurt: You feel betrayed and a victim of pain you didn't deserve.

Hate: You want revenge from the offender for the wrong he or she did to you.

Healing: You start to see the offender as a weak person who may use cruelty to cope with inadequacies.

Forgiveness: You begin to have positive thoughts; at first, perhaps, you only wish the person would reform; later you may want to consider a reconciliation.

"Unless we are willing to forgive,
we destroy the bridge whereby we receive
and perceive God's forgiveness of us."

Dr. David Seamands

Not long ago, my golfing friend, Huston Hall, brought me a tape of Adolph Coors' personal testimony. Coors grew up in the Colorado mountains where his father built the Coors Beer Company into a family fortune. Adolph related the story of his father's driving to the brewery from their snowy mountain home when he saw a stranded motorist and pulled over to the side of the road. Unwittingly, Coors had walked into a deadly trap. The supposed stranded traveler was, in fact, a murderous kidnapper. He killed Adolph's father and attempted to extort money from the family through a ransom note, but his plot was discovered and he eventually went to prison. Adolph confessed that this childhood event caused so much bitterness and hatred that it tainted his adult life. Coors testified that as his marriage, career and family crumbled around him, he sought forgiveness through the shed blood of Jesus Christ. Coors, who became a Christian, began to put Ephesians 4 into practice. Ultimately, Adolph Coors went to the prison cell that held his father's murderer and forgave him. What relief he experienced through this difficult experience!

> *"The weak can never forgive.*
> *Forgiveness is the attribute of the strong."*
> Mohandas K. Gandhi

While attending the National Association of Religious Broadcasters, I heard Senator Mark Hatfield recount the following story:

James Garfield was a lay preacher and principal of his denominational college. They say he was ambidextrous and could simultaneously write Greek with one hand and Latin with the other.

In 1880, he was elected president of the United States, but after only six months in office, he was shot in the back with a revolver. He never lost consciousness. At the hospital, the doctor probed the wound with his little finger to seek the bullet. He couldn't find it, so he tried a silver–tipped probe. Still he couldn't locate the bullet.

They took Garfield back to Washington, D.C. Despite the summer heat, they tried to keep him comfortable. He was growing very weak. Teams of doctors tried to locate the bullet, probing the wound over and over. In desperation they asked Alexander Graham Bell, who was working on a little device called the telephone to see if he could locate the metal inside the president's body. He came, he sought, and he too failed.

The president hung on through July, through August, but in September he finally died — not from the wound, but from infection. The repeated probing, which the physicians thought would help the man, eventually killed him.

So it is with people who refuse to forgive and harbor hateful feelings. Eventually, these feelings will kill the human spirit!

One of my favorite Peanuts cartoon strips depicts Lucy chasing Charlie Brown around and around the house. "I'll get you, Charlie Brown, I'll get you!" Suddenly, Charlie Brown stops. Lucy comes to a screeching stop.

Charlie Brown says, "If we, who are children, cannot forgive one another, how can we expect our parents, who are adults, to forgive one another, and in turn, how can the world...." At this point, Lucy punches Charlie Brown in the nose and knocks him down. Turning to a friend who had just come up, Lucy explains: "I had to hit him, he was beginning to make sense."[4]

Forgiving Others Brings Peace

Noted counselor and author, Dr. J. Allan Peterson, told the story of a woman who came to his office full of hatred for her husband. She told Dr. Peterson, "Before I divorce him, I want to hurt him as much as he has hurt me!"

Dr. Peterson encouraged the woman to return home and try to demonstrate love and forgiveness for 30 days. Additionally, he told her that if after 30 days of effort she still disliked him, she should consider a separation.

The woman went home and made an effort to praise her husband instead of picking at him. She decided to be helpful instead of difficult. And she began daily to express her love for him instead of hatred.

When she returned to Dr. Peterson's office after 30 days, the woman was beaming. Full of joy and enthusiasm, she said, "I don't want a divorce. I love this man!" She confessed that their relationship was healed through love, listening, giving and forgiving.

> *"It seems God is limited by our prayer life—*
> *that He can do nothing for humanity*
> *unless someone asks Him.*
>> John Wesley

Several years ago, I attended a service where my friend, Dr. H.B. London, Jr., now assistant to the president of Focus on the Family, was preaching. As we entered the sanctuary, each attendee received a brown paper lunch bag that was labeled "God Bag." Additionally, white strips of paper were distributed to each person. As Dr. London concluded his powerful message, he asked each person in attendance to write down his/her hurts, problems, and needs and put them in the God Bag. I joined with others in making my list.

One hurt was especially painful to write down. A person whom I had employed and had trusted as a friend had betrayed me. It appeared that the lie that had been told on me would never be corrected. Because it raised questions about my integrity, I was especially hurt and upset. Day after day, I thought about the incident, often weeping bitterly in prayer, asking God to deal with my offender. Finally, Dr. London instructed each person to prayerfully commit each concern to the Lord and to remove the strips of paper only as our prayers were answered. With a sense of relief and childlike faith, I placed my concerns into the God Bag. I felt better immediately! (Yes, even about my offender.)

Daily I began praying the Lord's Prayer. In that prayer, Jesus taught us to pray, "Forgive us our debts as we forgive our debtors." I chose not to curse or rehearse my hurts. I cupped my hands before the Lord and symbolically gave them over to God. I then raised my hands in prayer (both hands — pretty good for a Nazarene!) and claimed victory over my hurts!

Time passed and with each answer to prayer, I removed a strip of paper and gave thanks to God. Five years passed, and all but one strip of paper had been removed. You guessed it — there had been no contact from my offender. Then, one Saturday evening as I sat putting the finishing touches on my Sunday morning message titled, "What Is Forgiveness?" the phone rang. It was the person who had attacked my credibility.

The tearful voice said, "It's been years since I've talked to you. Will you forgive me for lying about you? Christ has forgiven me, and now I need to know — Stan, will you forgive me?" Without hesitation, I said, "You have my forgiveness!" What peace flooded my soul as I went to my office and took out the last strip of paper from the God Bag! God is never late in matters of forgiveness. He knows the very moment that our souls need relief!

I want to recommend several action steps to assist you in finding healing for your hurts.

Action Steps to Forgiveness

1. List the names of people who have offended you.

2. Place their names in a God Bag.

3. Pray daily for each offender by name.

4. Ask God to forgive you for the spirit of unforgiveness. Matthew 9:2 — *"Take heart...your sins are forgiven."*

5. Meditate on the following verses:

   "No longer will a man teach his neighbor, or a man his brother, saying, 'Know the Lord,' because they will all know me, from the least of them to the greatest,' declares the Lord. 'For I will forgive their wickedness and will remember their sins no more' Jeremiah 31:34.

   'But I tell you, do not resist an evil person. If someone strikes you on the right cheek, turn to him the other also' Matthew 5:39.

   'But I tell you: Love your enemies and pray for those who persecute you...' Matthew 5:44.

   "Do not judge, and you will not be judged. Do not condemn, and you will not be condemned. Forgive, and you will be forgiven" Luke 6:37.

   "Get rid of all bitterness, rage and anger, brawling and slander, along with every form of malice. Be kind and compassionate to one another, forgiving each other, just as in Christ God forgave you" Ephesians 4:31, 32.

Legend tells us that the beautiful Helen of Troy, over whom many battles were fought, was lost after one of the battles. When the army returned to Greece, Helen was not on any of the ships. Menelaus went to try and find her, at great personal peril. He finally found her in one of the seaport villages. She had been suffering from amnesia. Forgetting who she was, she had stooped to the lowest possible level and was living as a prostitute.

Menelaus found her in rags, dirt, shame, and dishonor. He looked at her and called, "Helen." Her head turned. "You are Helen of Troy!" he said. And with those words, her back straightened and the royal look came back. She had been redeemed and forgiven.

6.   Make a commitment "to forgive as Christ has forgiven you..."

7.   Take a step toward repairing a fractured relationship.

A recent "20/20" news segment told the story of Katherine Ann Power, who confessed her role in a 1970 bank robbery in which Officer Walter Schroeder was killed. What a frightening tale of teen rebellion she unfolded.

On September 17, 1993, the New York Times carried an interview story with the nephew of Officer Schroeder. The attitude of forgiveness and reconciliation was evident in the words of Officer Schroeder's nephew.

"I was very angry back then. If you had asked me then, I would have said, "Put her up against the wall and shoot her. I would have loved to have taken her to my aunt's house to show her what she did to those nine children." But as the interview continued, Mr. Schroeder said, "I find myself forgiving Ms. Powers now. For 49 years, I was taught to forgive — by my church, by my father. It gets imbedded in you more and more as you get older. There's no use in hating people."

General Oglethorpe once said to John Wesley,
"I never forgive and I never forget."
To which Wesley responded,
"Then, Sir, I hope you never sin."

[1]Rick Warren, *The Power to Change Your Life,* (Wheaton: Victor Books, 1990), p. 9.

[2]Neil Anderson, "The Bondage Breaker", *Spirit of Revival,* August 1993, pp. 8, 9.

[3]Craig Larson, Editor, *Illustrations for Preaching and Teaching,* (Grand Rapids: Baker Books, 1993).

[4]Rheta Grimsley Johnson, *Good Grief, the Story of Charles M. Schultz,* (New York: Pharos Books, 1989), p. 46.

10

Okay, God, If You're Listening, Why Aren't You Answering?

I heard a cute story about two nuns who were delivering medical supplies to a nursing home when their car ran out of gas. They searched in the trunk of the car for a gas can, but could only find a bedpan. The sisters walked a half mile to a gas station and filled the bedpan with gas.

Upon returning to their car, they carefully balanced the bedpan and started to pour the gas into the tank. About that time a man driving a pick–up truck approached, and as he saw what was going on, he came to a complete stop. Marveled at what he *thought* he was seeing, he stuck his head out of the truck window and said, "Sisters, I'm not Catholic, but I'll tell you what. I sure do admire your faith!"

The word of God clearly promises that God hears and answers our prayers, but at times, it appears that He is not listening. Why is it that some of our prayers seem to get through to God and yet other prayers seem to fall on deaf ears?

There are no easy answers, says Dr. James Dobson in *When God Doesn't Make Sense*. In 1987, four of Dr. Dobson's best friends were killed in a plane crash on their way home from a Focus on the Family retreat in Montana. Why did they have to die, leaving wives and children to carry on alone?

Dobson mentioned that life is filled with many examples of unexplainable pain and suffering brought upon godly people. Are these events evidence of God's wrath or something else? How do we explain these tragedies and others that strike both Christian and non–Christian alike? The Lord has not made it clear in the Bible why these things happen. What His Word does tell us is that we lack the capacity to understand God's infinite mind or the way He chooses to intervene in our lives.

"It is an incorrect view of Scripture to say that we will always comprehend what God is doing and how our suffering and disappointment fit into His plan," says Dobson. It is this *confusion* that shreds one's faith.

Expectations, Dobson writes, set us up for disillusionment. There's no greater distress than to build one's entire life around certain theological beliefs and then have those beliefs collapse when tragedy strikes.

Dr. Dobson gives four principles he's learned over the years about God's working in our lives:

1. God is present and involved in our lives even when He seems deaf or absent.

2. God's timing is perfect, even when He appears catastrophically late.

3. For reasons that are impossible to explain, we human beings are incredibly precious to God.

4. Our arms are too short to box with God. Don't even try.[1]

Dobson then tells hurting readers to expect confusing circumstances and to embrace them as opportunities for faith to grow.

After reading Dr. Dobson's book, my mind drifted back 12 years to the events surrounding the birth of our youngest son, Adam.

I had just closed my eyes for a brief afternoon nap. The conference in Dayton, Ohio, where I was speaking had seemingly drained all the energy out of me. The phone rang, disturbing my sleep. The caller encouraged me to hurry to the Fayette County Hospital where my wife, Linda, had gone into labor. Moments after I arrived, Adam James Toler was born into the world prematurely, weighing a whopping 8 pounds and 10 ounces!

As I pillowed my head just after midnight, I began to focus on the Sunday morning service at Heritage Memorial Church. I was tired but anxious to tell the congregation about the birth of our second son. The phone rang at 4:00 a.m. It was the doctor; "Come to the hospital quickly, Adam is having some difficulty," he said. I hustled to get dressed and rushed to the hospital in record time!

I noticed that the infant care mobile unit from Children's Hospital was parked at the emergency entrance of the Fayette County Hospital. Nurses met me at the door to explain that they had performed emergency surgery, and it would be necessary to take Adam to the Columbus Children's Hospital. After meeting with Dr. Chang, we agreed that Adam needed a moment to bond with his mother before leaving the hospital. Due to an infection that had developed, and because of Adam's difficulty in breathing, the two had not yet experienced a mother–son moment. As the nurse lifted Adam from his isolette unit and presented him to his mother for the first time, hot tears poured from my eyes. Watching Linda hold Adam for the first time and realizing that he might not live for another hour was overwhelming. Linda kissed Adam goodbye and watched intently as they rolled his isolette chamber from the room. I hugged Linda, and our tears mingled with the haunting thought that our son may not live through the day.

"Linda," I said, "Who pastors the pastor? All these years of ministry, I have stood by and encouraged others. I've prayed the prayers of comfort for many families, and here we are alone!" Linda pulled me down close and prayed a beautiful prayer of thanks for Adam and boldly asked God for a miracle.

> *"Sometimes God calms the raging storm.*
> *Sometimes He lets the storm rage*
> *and calms His child."*[2]
> Barbara Johnson

Driving to Children's Hospital in Columbus, Ohio, gave me time for thought and prayer. I pulled myself together, followed the medical team to the Infant Care Unit on the second floor and braced myself for the worst.

To my surprise, there were more than 30 premature infants in the Infant Care Unit at Children's Hospital. Some of the babies weighed less than 2 lbs and were smaller than my hand. Adam, at 8 lb. 10 oz., looked like a "giant among mortals." But he was a sick child. Doctors had determined that he had been born with a collapsed lung and was in serious condition.

Days and hours passed by. To my surprise, my church family was gracious and caring. They watched over Linda in the Fayette County Hospital, made arrangements for my in–laws, James and Nadine Carter, to come to Ohio from South Georgia to watch over our 4-year-old, Seth. They conducted daily prayer vigils at the church and visited me regularly at the hospital. During all of their care–giving, I began to realize the importance of lay ministry and discovered that lay persons can pastor the pastor!

Adam was strapped down, tubes running everywhere and always flat on his back. He rarely moved or made a sound. My job at the hospital was to be near him and to constantly touch him. It was the nurses' view that a parent's touch was very important to the recovery of the child. I couldn't agree more. The healing of those touches was going both directions.

On the third day, after taking a short lunch break, I returned to the Infant Care Unit only to encounter nurses who explained that Adam had taken a turn for the worse. "He may not live through the day," they said. Because they were performing emergency procedures, I was not allowed to be in the room. Hurriedly, I went to a phone and began to call friends from California to Virginia, asking them to pray for Adam. Hundreds gathered at Heritage Memorial Church for prayer. Heaven was being bombarded for Adam James!

Two hours passed, and a nurse came to get me. There was a weak feeling that went through my inner being. I was not optimistic. As I approached Adam, I noticed that he was face down on the bed, no diaper, his rear end sticking up in the air, and there was movement! I asked the nurse, "What does this mean?"

"Pastor," she explained, "It's the 'Butt' sign."

"The butt sign?" I inquired.

"Yes, sir," she explained. "When we turn them over on their tummy, it means they are going to make it! Sir, your prayers have been answered. You have a healthy son and he'll be going home soon!"

I was in a state of shock. "God has healed my son," I cried. What rejoicing I felt that day. How ashamed I was of my own lack of faith, and yet how thrilled I was at the faith of my brothers and sisters in Christ. They had touched God for me!

God is never late when you need a miracle!

Release Your Faith Right Now!

Does it seem like your prayers are not being answered? Release your faith right now and believe that God in heaven hears and answers prayer!

"God's promise is as
good as His presence."

Andrew Murray

Faith-Building Exercises

"*Now faith is being sure of what we hope for and certain of what we do not see. This is what the ancients were commended for*" Hebrews 11:1, 2. The Word of God mentions the words *faith* or *believe* 485 times. It occurs 23 times in the 11th chapter of Hebrews alone.

As I conclude this book, let me give you seven important steps to faith–building. While it is true, "God has never failed me," it is also a reality that I have practiced the following faith principles.

STEP ONE: Study the promises of God.

Award-winning author Philip Yancey described two kinds of faith in an article entitled, *"When God Seems Silent."* First, Yancey discussed seed faith as the David–meeting–Goliath-"with God all things are possible"-kind of faith. Secondly, he talks about fidelity — the "hang on at any cost" faith like that of Job.[4]

In my opinion, both faith systems work. Fred Price uses the metaphor of flying an airplane. The life of victory is a matter of *"walking by faith, not by sight"* 2 Corinthians 5:7. It's a matter of flying by the instruments — by the word of God — when the fog is so heavy we can't see out the windows of our aircraft. It's a matter of fighting the good fight of faith — but we go into the ring already knowing who wins."[5] We must leave the realm of our senses and make our spiritual reference point the promises of God.

For a real faith–lift, review daily the promises of God. Listed below are a few promises that have helped me immensely:

God promises to hear my prayers. *"Before they call I will answer; while they are still speaking I will hear"* Isaiah 65:24.

God promises to reward my faithfulness. *"For the Son of Man is going to come in his Father's glory with his angels, and then he will reward each person according to what he has done"* Matthew 16:27.

God promises His presence in my life. *"...and teaching them to obey everything I have commanded you. And surely I will be with you always, to the very end of the age"* Matthew 28:20.

God promises to help me when I call. *"All that the Father gives me will come to me, and whoever comes to me I will never drive away"* John 6:37.

God promises to turn my tears into triumphs. *"And we know that in all things God works for the good of those who love him, who have been called according to his purpose"* Romans 8:28.

God promises to put an end to sin and death. *"He will wipe every tear from their eyes. There will be no more death or mourning or crying or pain, for the old order of things has passed away"* Revelation 21:4.

Our faith connects us with God. Ruth Vaughn, quoting her mother, said, " You must have deep within you the consciousness that there is a God, that He loves you, and that you are in His hands."[6] This can only happen when our faith is based on God's promises.

> *"Every promise in the Book is mine,*
> *Every chapter, every verse, every line.*
> *And I'm living in His love divine,*
> *Every promise in the Book is mine."*
>
> John Bayman

STEP TWO: Demonstrate Faithful Obedience to God.

John Wesley once said, "God has appointed faith to supply the defect of sense, to take us up where sense lets us down, and to help us over the gulf." Faith grows from that of a servant, with *obedience* based in fear, to that of a son who obeys God out of love.

When God sees our faithful obedience in the most difficult times, He promises to see us through!

"Remember those earlier days after you had received the light, when you stood your ground in a great contest in the face of suffering.

Sometimes you were publicly exposed to insult and persecution; at other times you stood side by side with those who were so treated. You sympathized with those in prison and joyfully accepted the confiscation of your property, because you knew that you yourselves had better and lasting possessions Hebrews 10:32-24.

Rebecca Olson, in an article for *Decision* magazine, said, The story of Noah is an example of the truth that the crowd is often wrong. Noah stood against public opinion for 120 years because his heart and mind were set on a predetermined course: one that he believed in fully. Another reason was that his outward life matched his convictions; he practiced what he preached. Noah was also assured of success because he knew the master plan.

Noah realized he was the one to influence the crowd, rather than the one who was influenced by it. He established a priority and then for 120 years day after day, his hands built the Ark while his mouth proclaimed salvation. To stand against a crowd, and for Jesus, requires courage, action, a consistent life, obedience, and a knowledge of God's clear instructions.[7]

STEP THREE: Spend Time with People of Faith.

Even Jesus Christ was careful to resist the influence of unbelievers. Christians must be careful to resist the vain philosophies, values and unbeliefs of the non–Christian. We must surround ourselves with people of faith.

"So do not throw away your confidence; it will be richly rewarded. You need to persevere so that when you have done the will of God, you will receive what he has promised. For in just a very little while, "He who is coming will come and will not delay. But my righteous one will live by faith. And if he shrinks back, I will not be pleased with him.

But we are not of those who shrink back and are destroyed, but of those who believe and are saved" Hebrews 10:35-39.

For years now I have intentionally spent time with positive people. Don't spend your time with pessimistic people if you need a faith–lift!

Lightning flashed outside the windows as the little girl crept into her parents' bedroom and shook her mother awake, "I'm scared."

"What?" asked the groggy mom.

"I'm scared, and I want to sleep with you." Somewhat more awake now, the mother gave her daughter a gentle hug and tried to comfort her.

"There's nothing to be afraid of. It's just a storm. Everything is OK. Now, you go on back to your bedroom and remember God will be there with you in your bed."

The small figure stood in the dark for a long moment and then said, "Mom, how about if you go sleep in there with God, and I'll sleep in here with Daddy."

STEP FOUR: Seek the Gift of Faith in Prayer.

"At once Jesus realized that power had gone out from him. He turned around in the crowd and asked, 'Who touched my clothes?' 'You see the people crowded against you,' his disciples answered, 'and yet you can ask, 'Who touched me?'"

But Jesus kept looking around to see who had done it Mark 5:30-32.

The woman who reached out to touch Jesus brings us to the realization that the best way to secure a mountain–moving faith relationship with God is through your obedience to Him in the little things of life. It is "faith the size of a mustard seed" that grows through the circumstances of life that brings us to the gift of faith. Every day by faith claim this wonderful gift from God!

My faith looks up to Thee,
Thou Lamb of Calvary, Savior divine!
Now hear me while I pray;
Take all my guilt away.
O let me from this day Be wholly Thine![7]

STEP FIVE: Read Biographies of Faithful Christians.

I have been reading biographies of great people since I was in grade school. People of faith stretch me mightily in my relationship with the Lord. Over the years, I have enjoyed reading biographies of Bresee, Moody, Wesley, Asbury, and Mueller.

God is the great I am.
Am is in the present tense.
He is ready to do it now,
so when you pray, believe that
the promises of God are
yea and amen in Christ Jesus.
Buddy Harrison

I especially enjoyed reading about George Mueller, one of my heroes in the faith. The following story about Mueller's faith is my personal favorite.

George Mueller of Bristol received more than $1 million for his children's orphanage over a 60-year period. He never asked for a penny; rather, he always prayed it in!

The captain of a ship on which George Mueller was sailing told the story of a trip on which there was a very dense fog, and the captain was on the bridge for 24 hours, without ever leaving the helm. Mr. Mueller came to him and said, "Captain, I have come to tell you that I must be in Quebec on Saturday afternoon."

The captain replied, "It is impossible."

"Very well, then," Mr. Mueller said, "if your ship cannot take me, God will find another way. I have never broken an engagement in 57 years, and I won't start now. Let's go down into the chart room and pray."

The captain looked at Mr. Mueller and thought, What a lunatic! I've never heard of such..."Mr. Mueller," he said, "do you know how dense this fog is?"

"No," he said, "my eye is not on the density of the fog, but on the living God who controls every circumstance of my life!" He knelt down and prayed a simple prayer. When he finished, the captain knelt to pray, but Mr. Mueller put his hand on the captain's shoulder and said, "Since you do not believe, don't pray. God will answer, Captain. I've known my Lord for 57 years. There has never been a day when I failed to get an audience with the King."

"Get up, Captain. Open the door and you will find the fog has gone!" The captain got up, opened the door and saw that indeed the fog was gone. And on that very Saturday afternoon, George Mueller kept his engagement!

> *"Faith is like radar that sees through the fog —*
> *the reality of things at a distance*
> *that the human eye cannot see."*
> Corrie Ten Boom

STEP SIX: Testify of Your Faith in Christ.

"So the man went away and began to tell in Decapolis how much Jesus had done for him. And all the people were amazed Mark 5:20.

I loved the enthusiasm of one of my young teenage converts who wanted to be baptized. He said, "Pastor, I want to get *advertised!*" Excitement about your faith in Christ is contagious. Fulfill the great commission by testifying of your faith in Christ.

THE GREAT COMMISSION

Therefore go and make disciples of all nations,
baptizing them in the name of the
Father and of the Son and of the Holy Spirit,
and teaching them to obey everything I have
commanded you. And surely I will
be with you always, to the very end of the age.

Matthew 28:19, 20

It is important to share the miracle of salvation with your family and friends. A relationship with Christ is fundamental to His miraculous intervention in our lives.

STEP SEVEN: Expect Results!

"Jesus looked at them and said, 'With man this is impossible, but with God all things are possible'" Matthew 19:26.

While watching "CNN News" recently, I was fascinated by an interview with a man who wanted to fly and inadvertently stopped air traffic near the Los Angeles Airport. This innovative man came up with the idea of flying over his community. After anchoring his lawn chair with sturdy rope, he tied helium-filled balloons to the arm rests. He packed himself a nice lunch to enjoy while flying over his neighborhood and then strapped himself into the chair with a makeshift seat belt. Additionally, he tied on a BB gun to shoot the balloons when he began his descent back to earth.

"I cut the anchor ropes loose and expected to go about one thousand feet in the air, but instead I shot up 11,000 feet into the air!" he exclaimed. This action launched him into the traffic pattern of LAX, and it took an Air Force helicopter to get him down! The interviewer's final question amused me greatly. "Sir, were you scared?" he asked the weary navigator.

"Yes, I was, but wonderfully so!"

What a wonderful story! As I reflected on what took place, I began to think. A balloon filled with helium is lighter than air. The balloon takes on the characteristic of that which fills it. Believers take on the quality of Christ when filled with the Holy Spirit. When He takes control of your life, you identify His traits. When He dwells in you, you become more bouyant and able to rise above the circumstances of life.

And now I ask you, if God performed a miracle in your life, would you be scared? Let me answer for you. Yes, you would! But wonderfully so. *God has never failed me, but He's scared me to death a few times!*

[1]James Dobson, *When God Doesn't Make Sense,* (Wheaton: Tyndale House Publishers, 1993), pp. 45-63.

[2]Barbara Johnson, *Mama, Get the Hammer! There's A Fly on Papa's Head,* (Dallas: Word Publishing, 1994).

[3]"My Faith Looks Up to Thee," (Words: Ray Palmer, 1830; Music: Lowell Mason, 1832), Public Domain.

[4]Philip Yancey, "When God Seems Silent," *Today's Christian Woman,* March/April 1989, pp. 28-30.

[5]Fred Price, "Keeping the Faith," *Charisma and Christian Life,* October 1988, pp. 58-63.

[6]Ruth Vaughn, (Moody), December 1988, pp. 60-62.

[7]Rebecca Olson, "Building for Life," *Decision,* November 1987, pp. 33-35.

About The Author

Dr. Stan Toler currently serves as Pastor-in-Residence at Southern Nazarene University in Bethany, Oklahoma, and is Vice President of INJOY Ministries located in San Diego, California. Stan has touched hundreds of lives with his "INJOY "Model Church Seminars" and is widely known as a "Pastor to Pastors."

Prior to accepting the position at Southern Nazarene University, Stan served as Senior Pastor in four growing Nazarene churches across the United States. His most recent assignment was at the historic 2,000 member First Church of the Nazarene located in Nashville, Tennessee. Prior to his 26 years of pastoral experience Dr. Toler served at Circleville Bible College and Florida Beacon as Professor of Homiletics, Systematic Theology, and Greek.

Other published works and manuals by Dr. Toler include:

Essentials to Evangelism

75 Years of Powerful Preaching

Proven Principles of Stewardship

Lessons for Growing Christians

A History of the Oklahoma City First Church of the Nazarene

Church Empowerment Manual

Minister's LIttle Instruction Book

ABC's of Evangelism

104 Sermons — Co-Authored with John Maxwell

Pastor's Guide to Celebrations and Events

Team Building

Honor Books, Inc.
Tulsa, OK 74155